Praise for *The Faci...*
Blended, a...

"Through detailed examples and advice from experts in the field, Cindy Huggett lays out an invaluable approach to delivering highly immersive learning solutions. Her ability to clarify and simplify brings instant applicability to modern learning design."

—Brandon Carson, VP of Learning, Walmart

"This book is a must-have for your learning and development bookshelf. Not only will you pick up tips for how to design and deliver incredible digital training, you'll want to use these strategies for all your training programs!"

—Kassy LaBorie, Co-Author, *Interact and Engage! 75+ Activities for Virtual Training, Meetings, and Webinars*, Second Edition

"Cindy has once again provided a cutting-edge book to help us understand a critical new direction in learning and development. The chart in chapter 1 comparing the traditional trainer versus the learning experience facilitator is eye opening. And her troubleshooting chart for VR helps us prepare for the hiccups that will surely come. This book is one of my top 10 for the year."

—Bob Pike, 2021 ATD Lifetime Achievement Award winner; Chairman, CTT Press

"Whether she's sharing a personal story or providing priceless tips, Cindy draws you into her world of immersive, blended, and hybrid learning. Her step-by-step process to move from a traditional trainer to a learning experience facilitator is on target. And her guidance to get you there is definitive."

—Elaine Biech, 2022 ISA Thought Leader; Author, *The Art and Science of Training* and *ATD's Handbook for Training and Talent Development*

The Facilitator's Guide to **Immersive, Blended,** and **Hybrid Learning**

Cindy Huggett

atd
PRESS
Alexandria, VA

25 24 23 22   1 2 3 4 5

ATD Press is an internationally renowned source of insightful and practical information on talent development, training, and professional development.

ATD Press
1640 King Street
Alexandria, VA 22314 USA

Ordering information: Books published by ATD Press can be purchased by visiting ATD's website at td.org/books or by calling 800.628.2783 or 703.683.8100.

Library of Congress Control Number: 2022943363

ISBN-10: 1-950496-69-4
ISBN-13: 978-1-950496-69-3
e-ISBN: 978-1-950496-70-9

ATD Press Editorial Staff
Director: Sarah Halgas
Manager: Melissa Jones
Content Manager, Learning Technology: Alexandria Clapp
Developmental Editor: Hannah Sternberg
Text Design: Shirley E.M. Raybuck
Cover Design: Rose Richey
Text Layout: PerfecType, Nashville, TN

Printed by BR Printers, San Jose, CA

Contents

Introduction

Immersive experiences are increasingly permeating everyday life. In January 2018, I attended the ATD TechKnowledge Conference in West Palm Beach, Florida. It was a typical conference full of networking with colleagues, listening to exciting keynote speakers, and attending education sessions. The Florida sunshine allowed us to get outdoors between sessions and explore the surrounding areas.

There was a shopping complex near the convention center filled with unique stores and restaurants. As I wandered over for a quick break, I had no idea what a momentous decision it would be, because I stumbled upon the traveling *Downton Abbey* exhibit, which was on its first US stop. I was a huge fan of this popular television show and immediately got a ticket and went inside. I thought it would be fun to see the costumes and learn more about the production. From the moment I walked in the door, I was captivated.

To my surprise, it wasn't just an *ordinary* museum exhibit; it was *extraordinary*. I felt like I was stepping onto a TV set. The characters and the show came to life. The robust exhibit mixed technology with trivia in a way that I'd personally never before experienced.

The first room was filled with a maze of full-screen video panels featuring each character. The next rooms replicated other aspects of the show, and the minute details were incredible. But the exhibit did more than just replicate the set; it was *immersive*. I stood in the Crawleys' living room while scenes from the show took place around me. The kitchen came alive with Mrs. Pattmore's baked goods. I walked into the dining room just before a dinner was about to be served, and it was as if I were actually there. I heard the voices, I saw the imagery, and I felt the emotion.

It was an exhilarating experience I would not forget—partly because I loved the show, and partly because it opened my mind to possibilities. The combination of being at a training conference focused on technology and attending this entrancing museum exhibit led me to explore immersive learning. That specific experience stimulated my thinking and formed the foundations of this book.

Around this same time, I discovered early versions of immersive experiences integrating into virtual classrooms. With my consulting emphasis on upskilling virtual trainers, I wondered about the impact of these new tools on facilitators. I wanted to know how to prepare facilitators to incorporate these new tools into their virtual classes, and what updated skills they would need. My interest in this question led me down the research trail of immersive technologies in all learning environments.

Immersive and Other New Learning Environments

To be clear, immersive learning isn't new—it is an educational experience that engrosses the learner in a realistic environment for the purposes of knowledge and skill building. Simulated training experiences, a form of immersive learning, have been around since at least the 1700s, when the French Academy of Surgeons approved a childbirth simulator created by Madame du Coudray, a midwife for King Louis XV. She traveled the countryside using experiential techniques to teach midwives about childbirth, and subsequent infant mortality rates dropped (Walton 2017).

Many other examples of simulations and experiential learning can be found across a multitude of industries. From military training exercises to apprenticeship programs, replicating the real world in a learning context is a common endeavor. Even technology-based immersive learning experiences, such as airplane pilot training simulators, have also been around for decades.

Yet we are at an interesting time in history due to the rapid integration of technology into our everyday lives. Updates in the quality, accessibility, and features of technology have created new opportunities for learning. In addition, thanks to a notable digital shift in our industry, learning opportunities now go beyond traditional training simulations.

For example, smartphone use is at an all-time high and continuing to grow. In 2021, 85 percent of all Americans had a smartphone, which is a massive increase from just 35 percent in 2011 (Pew Research 2021). Smartphones allow for on-the-go learning, enabling access to training anytime and anywhere. They contribute to immersive learning by acting as the lens for augmented reality (AR) applications.

Wearables, like smart watches and other jewelry, are also becoming more widespread. In fact, about one in five Americans regularly wears some type of smart watch or other connected fitness tracker (Vogels 2020). This everyday adoption opens the door of acceptance to other smart, internet-connected products and wearables, like glasses, goggles, and headsets.

In 2020, the COVID-19 pandemic changed workplace dynamics worldwide. Most organizations rapidly transitioned their traditional classes to online learning experiences. Organizations needed to quickly search for ways to leverage technology, increase reach to remote learners, and create flexible programs. And in the process, the role of trainers and facilitators changed.

What's the facilitator role in these new immersive, virtual, blended, and hybrid learning environments? What traditional trainer skills apply, and what new skills are needed in these technology-driven learning environments? When is a facilitator needed to enable learning, and what do they do to drive learning results? These are the key questions we will answer in this book.

About This Book

This book is by a facilitator, for facilitators. I am a lifelong teacher, trainer, and educator—I've been doing it since I was four years old, when I'd set my dolls in front of an old blackboard every day and teach them everything I'd learned. Many of those who feel drawn to this role feel that same excitement about learning. It's a part of who we are. We love being in the classroom—both in person and online—and are continually trying to improve our skills.

In addition to the facilitation skills and techniques that I use in my own training projects, this book also features experiences and stories from many of my colleagues and clients. You will read about their real-world experience, discover their lessons learned, and hear their advice.

If you are not a facilitator and are instead an instructional designer, course developer, learning consultant, training manager, measurement specialist, or any other training department role, don't despair. While the primary audience is facilitators, everyone can glean important information from the discussion. Facilitators rarely operate in a vacuum, and roles overlap. For example, designers and developers create the learning experiences that trainers facilitate. And training managers make business decisions that directly affect a trainer's work. We all need to incorporate the new principles of immersive facilitation in what we do, at each level of learning development and management.

This book will walk you through the world of immersive, virtual, blended, and hybrid learning, step by step. Let's take a closer look at what we'll cover in each chapter:

▶ **Chapter 1. The New Learning Experience Facilitator**—The book begins by diving deep into the role the facilitator plays in any learning environment. It introduces a new term, the *learning experience facilitator*, by explaining each word—*learning, experience,* and *facilitator*—and what happens in the facilitator role when you combine those definitions.

▶ **Chapter 2. Technology for Immersive Learning**—This chapter clearly explains current technologies used in learning environments, including virtual classrooms, blended learning, virtual reality (VR), augmented reality (AR), and mixed reality (MR). Think of it as a primer, full of definitions and explanations.

▶ **Chapter 3. Facilitating Immersive Virtual Classes**—In this chapter, we will explore new developments in live online learning. I also share practical facilitator techniques you can use to engage remote learners in the virtual classroom. This content will likely feel the most familiar to facilitators who have already been using online collaboration tools to connect with dispersed audiences.

- **Chapter 4. Facilitating Hybrid Classes**—This chapter provides the essential skills needed to facilitate effectively when some participants are in the room and others are remote. This hybrid audience model exploded in popularity in the post-pandemic business world, so we will look at the skills required to do it well.

- **Chapter 5. Facilitating Blended Learning Journeys**—This chapter considers the importance of the facilitator's role in blended training curriculums, in which the facilitator acts as guide and enabler throughout a learning journey. We'll look at the best practices for facilitator involvement outside the traditional classroom, and how to keep learners motivated throughout.

- **Chapter 6: Facilitating With Augmented Reality**—Because AR components can be easily incorporated into classroom experiences, this chapter explores the facilitator's roles and responsibilities in using these tools. It also provides examples of how to use them and tips for success.

- **Chapter 7. Facilitating With Virtual Reality**—This chapter answers the big questions: What does a facilitator do to lead participants in a VR training program? When is a facilitator needed inside the immersive experience? How does the facilitator add value? What skills are needed to enable learning?

- **Chapter 8. The Facilitator of the Future**—This final chapter serves as a springboard for "what's next" in facilitation. It considers newly emerging trends and offers advice to facilitators on how to stay current or even ahead of the curve.

Because the immersive learning landscape will undoubtedly continue to grow and change in the future, I've created a resource page on my website (cindyhuggett.com/facilitatorsguide) to help us all stay current on trends and to provide easy access to some of the ready-to-use items found in this book. My site also serves as a go-to place for your questions and comments about virtual training. I hope to hear from you and learn from your experiences as well!

CHAPTER 1

The New Learning Experience Facilitator

If you're looking for an instructional design job, it may be hard to find. Not because there aren't instructional design positions available, but because the new, *en vogue* job title is *Learning Experience Designer*. A quick search for this role on LinkedIn reveals thousands of results.

The term *learning experience design* has progressively creeped into the L&D lexicon over the past 20 years. According to e-learning expert Connie Malamed (2022), it was first mentioned in a 2002 article by Hillary McLellan. By 2020, many articles had been written about learning experience design in industry magazines, and it had become part of everyday vocabulary.

Even though the terminology is relatively new, the concepts have been assembled and espoused by learning thought leaders for almost a century. For example, the table of contents of Wilbert McKeachie's book *Teaching Tips*, first published in 1951, includes many components of learning experience design. Numerous other research studies, authors, blog posts, articles, and books have studied and expanded on the concepts. To use a gardening analogy, learning experience design has rooted, sprouted, and grown out of combined efforts from many elements over a long period of time.

What Is Learning Experience Design?

Collectively as an industry, we have not yet settled upon one official definition for learning experience design. It is still under debate whether it's an entirely new method of instructional design or just an evolution of traditional instructional design methods. I believe it's a combination of both: a new approach to designing learning solutions that honors the legacy of traditional instructional design processes (such as ADDIE) while incorporating more modern techniques (such as design thinking).

In short, *learning experience design (LXD)* is an interdisciplinary approach to designing learning that combines user experience theory and practices with learning research and instructional design principles. It pulls concepts from cognitive psychology, design thinking, and learning science.

LXD is particularly important in immersive, blended, and hybrid learning, where training is more than just the content presented—it's an intentional effort focusing on *how*, *why*, and *when* learning happens. In other words, the experience is what enables the learning outcomes.

A hallmark of learning experience design is that it's centered on the learner from start to finish. The "learner" is the person who needs to perform a workplace task or learn to behave in a certain way. Much like user experience design in the software industry, learning experience designers seek to submerge themselves in the learner's perspective so they can create ideal solutions. Learning experience designers empathize with their audience to craft an authentic experience that leads to learning outcomes and behavior change.

It's good to note that traditional instructional design, when done well, has always centered on the learner. For example, the first step in ADDIE—the most widely used instructional design model—is analysis. This is when the designer determines the goal, assesses the need, and defines the target audience. It confirms that training will achieve desired results and focuses on creating a relevant solution. But LXD goes one step further by keeping a laser focus solely on the learner throughout the entire design process.

The ADDIE model also leads most traditional instructional designers to create a single training solution, such as a course, a workshop, or an e-learning event. But LXD tends to dive deeper into the analysis phase, asking the designer to step back, determine if training is even the right solution, and often go further in audience analysis. They then blend more modern approaches, which are based on learning science, to create a multifaceted program instead of a single training solution.

The rise of LXD, in fact, is visible in the increased popularity of blended learning journeys. Well-designed learning journeys immerse learners in real-world situations, on-the-job scenarios, and practical application activities. They are baked into a learner's everyday reality, which creates a sense of continuous and relevant learning.

The Design–Delivery Connection

Let's back up for a moment and connect the dots between design and delivery. In the traditional ADDIE process to create an instructor-led course, the first thing to happen is that a need arises. That need is analyzed, and the result is a recommended learning solution. Then the learning solution is designed, and the program and its accompanying materials (including guides, graphics, activities, and handouts) are developed. Next the program is facilitated and finally evaluated for success. Most of these tasks are completed by a designer. Trainers get involved at the end of the development phase when the program is piloted, and they also carry out the facilitation and delivery tasks.

Of course, there are as many variations to this process as there are types of organizations. In smaller businesses the trainer and designer are often the same person. In larger ones, this process is often a team effort with multiple players. However, the actual number of people involved is much less important than the overall process—a relevant training solution is *designed* and then it's *delivered*.

ATD's Talent Development Capability Model (formerly the ATD Competency Model) includes *instructional design* and *training delivery and facilitation* as separate but related capabilities under the Building Professional Capability domain. While most learning professionals specialize in one or the other (or a different niche altogether), these two skill sets are intricately related. Trainers should know at least the basics of instructional design, and designers should be familiar with effective delivery techniques. Both are important capabilities for well-rounded learning professionals.

3 KEYS TO TRAINING SUCCESS

As I've noted extensively in my other books on virtual training, including *The Virtual Training Guidebook and Virtual Training Tools and Templates*, in addition to design and delivery, there is a third important factor in learning: the participants. This idea is supported in LXD, due to its focus on the learner. The three critical components of any successful learning experience are:

1. **Interactive design.** Training should intentionally engage the learner in meaningful activity that leads to the desired learning outcomes. This could range from classic role plays in breakout groups to a full-blown VR immersive experience.
2. **Engaging delivery.** Training must be delivered by skilled facilitators who invite learners into the dialogue instead of keeping the focus on themselves. Immersive facilitation relies more on collaboration than presentation.
3. **Prepared participants.** Training needs to be a priority for learners, who see the benefit of learning new skills and therefore take an active role in the process. They need to be properly equipped for learning, especially when technology is required for the learning experience.

In the train-the-trainer workshops I taught long ago, I would ask my students two questions: "Can a great facilitator carry a poorly designed training program?" and "Can a really well-designed training program make up for poor facilitation skills?"

These questions always sparked vigorous discussion among the group, with strong arguments made on both sides. However, the main takeaway was always focused on the intricate connection between the two components: design and delivery. The best learning experiences come from a well-designed program that's expertly delivered. Both are critical factors to success.

Because design and delivery are interconnected, like two sides of the same coin, when one goes through a transformation, so should the other. If instructional design evolves, so too must its related tasks, including facilitation. If the field of instructional design has morphed to learning experience design, incorporating immersive, blended, or hybrid elements, then the role of the trainer needs to update too. Let's take a closer look.

A Transformation and an Evolution

The rapid pace of change is mirrored in many industries, not just learning and development. For example, think of the internet. In the mid-1990s, the World Wide Web was a static experience of visiting informational online websites. Then came Web 2.0, which added interactions, ratings, and discussion. Now we are in the era of Web 3.0, which centers on user-created content and communities.

Likewise, computing devices have evolved over time. Personal desktop computers brought high-powered data to our stationary desks. Then came laptops, which allowed users to choose their working location because they were no longer tethered to one room. In today's era of mobile devices, we have small, powerful, handheld computers that fit in our back pocket. The idea of needing a static location to access data no longer exists; instead, it's ubiquitous and we are surrounded by it.

In a similar vein, we could argue that the trainer's role has already changed. First was the esteemed instructor—someone who imparted knowledge as a subject matter expert in a formal classroom. They lectured and presented, demonstrated skill in public speaking, and commanded respect as an authority on the topic.

Then came the rise of the trainer role. An expert classroom trainer was a "guide on the side" as well as a "sage on the stage" (King 1993). This person combined teaching and learning with exploration, as they expertly included participants in program activities. Skilled trainers managed classroom dynamics, weaving interaction into their teaching. Yet even in this atmosphere of activity, the trainer maintained control of the timing, logistics, and training space.

Over the past few years, we have moved squarely into promoting the facilitator's role in learning environments. Part of the reason for this shift is that workplace skills are becoming increasingly more complex and rote instruction isn't enough (Autor and Price 2013). Another reason is the increase in self-directed, individualized workforces, along with informal learning (Santos, Varnum, and Grossmann 2017; Shank 2016). A skilled facilitator enables participants to go through a learning process that leads to positive outcomes. In addition to formal classes with instruction and activity, there may also be self-directed exploration and application. The facilitator asks questions, provides guidance, and supports the overall learning experience.

This evolution from instructor to trainer to facilitator doesn't mean there isn't a place for instruction. Just as the internet still provides plenty of informational websites, and ultra-powerful desktop computers are still needed, so are instructors and educators. There is a time and place for subject matter experts to speak, and there are plentiful opportunities for them to share interesting presentations. The major challenge is when there's a mismatched solution—when lecture is provided but facilitation is needed.

The challenge for most instructors and trainers is to know when to let go of lecturing and focus on facilitating—to distinguish between when a presentation or demonstration is sufficient, and when the instructor needs to step back and allow the learner to lead. My hope is that this book will provide that pathway as learning programs become more immersive experiences.

This takes us back to the transformation of the instructional designer to the learning experience designer. If learning experiences are now the norm, if learning journeys are the new normal, and if modern workplace learning is expected, then the facilitator role must also adapt and change. It's time for a new name, new knowledge, new skills, new tools, and a new mindset.

The New Learning Experience Facilitator Role

So, if there's a new modern design role called the learning experience designer, then it makes sense that there should also be a new modern facilitator role, called the *learning experience facilitator.* To help set context and provide insight, let's review each part of this new name.

Learning

The dictionary describes *learning* as "the act or process of acquiring knowledge or skill." It comes from the Old English word *leornung,* which means "to learn, read, ponder." These definitions only scratch the surface of what's needed for workplace learning, which requires one more step: behavior change. To acquire knowledge is one thing; to act upon that knowledge is another.

Think of it this way: A retail associate may learn how to use a store's cash register to ring up a customer's purchase. They can navigate the system, enter the data, accept payment, and provide a receipt. These tasks are transactional knowledge. But what if problem-solving skills are required because a customer cites a price discrepancy or their coupon isn't working? Or what if the associate also needs to show empathy and strive to create a memorable customer experience? These elements are less transactional and more interpersonal. They require a deeper understanding of both the purchasing system and social dynamics. Routine knowledge usually isn't enough for this task; learning is needed.

Or consider your own career journey. How did you learn to do your current job? It was probably a process of learning, building skills, and discovering. You may have taken some formal classes, you may have had a mentor show you the ropes, and you likely learned a lot on your own. You found resources to support the information you needed when you needed it. Learning opportunities were all around you, and you accessed them at the right times.

Bob Mosher and Conrad Gottfredson's research on workflow learning provides an easy-to-understand framework for this immersive process.

Mosher describes it as "learning that occurs while I do my job" (as opposed to stopping work to engage in a learning activity; James 2020). Mosher and Gottfredson's research has found that people learn at five specific moments in time:

1. When learning something for the first time (learn new)
2. When expanding upon what they have learned (learn more)
3. When needing to act upon what they learned (apply)
4. When needing to problem solve when things don't go as planned (solve)
5. When unlearning old habits and relearning new approaches (change)

Note that these moments can all occur as someone is doing their job, immersed in their everyday tasks.

In summary, learning is more than acquiring knowledge; it's about applying that knowledge in the proper context. Most learning happens informally, when a person needs that specific information. Learning involves behavior change in the form of doing something or doing it better than before.

While it may seem like this description shifts all responsibility away from trainers and onto learners, that thinking couldn't be further from the truth. Instead, it supports the idea that facilitation plays a key role. The facilitator's role in supporting learning experiences has expanded—rather than simply delivering a lecture, facilitators enable learners and support the entire learning environment. Whether that environment is in a classroom or at a work site, a skilled facilitator helps create the conditions for learning to occur.

Experience

One of my clients asked me to create a set of editable resources for their instructional designers to use when transitioning from in-person to online classes. They had taken and loved my "Designing Virtual Learning for Engagement" online workshop, and wanted to capture the course content in job aids. However, when I worked up some draft documents for their review, their response was merely lukewarm. The right content was there, but the workshop experience was missing. They quickly realized that posting a set of job aids to the company intranet would be helpful, but those documents wouldn't replace the visceral experience of attending a live workshop with peers who collaborated on a design. It's difficult to replicate a 3-D experience in a 2-D document. What they really wanted was to re-create the overall learning environment.

Think about times you have been immersed in an experience: whether it was walking past a bakery through a cloud of fresh-from-the-oven cookie smells or being immersed in the perfect dining experience at a fancy restaurant, created by intentional choices in the color scheme, décor, and ambiance, you likely became engrossed in the atmosphere.

Experiences evoke emotion because they heighten the senses. That's why they help people learn. A single powerful experience can quickly change someone's behavior. (Like deciding to walk into the bakery because of the delicious smell wafting outside.) This is a main reason for using experience as a learning tool.

Experiential learning isn't new. David Kolb's experiential learning theory (ELT) has influenced workplace learning for decades (Kolb 1984). Many education programs incorporate experiential elements into their curriculums and have done so for years—student teaching for elementary school teachers, clinicals for nurse practitioners, and rotational programs for high-potential leaders are just a few examples. These experiences help bridge the gap between theory and practice, between the classroom and the real world.

Experiential learning also supports the idea of learning in context. Contextual learning asserts that people learn best when they can create meaning based on their experience (Hudson and Whisler 2008). In other words, a trainer could explain a new concept using a fictious ice cream analogy or a real-world scenario. While the ice cream analogy might not be bad, the real-world scenario would give the learners a better grasp of the concept. And even better, the trainer could facilitate a real-world activity so the learners discover the meaning of the new concept and how it relates to their work.

For example, imagine how new hotel managers learn to do their jobs. They could go to a training workshop at the hotel's headquarters, spend several weeks in a classroom to learn the details, and eventually return to their home property. Or, they could stay at their property and take a series of facilitator-led online workshops with relevant on-the-job application assignments placed between each session. The managers who immersively learn a new task and immediately get to apply it in the context of their workplace will have more effective learning experiences, and ultimately get better results.

Many training programs try to replicate real-world experiences through classroom simulation activities. Whether it's a simple role-play exercise or a complex case study scenario, the goal is for the learner to practice in a real-world setting. For example, one of my previous clients—a fast-food restaurant chain—went so far as to build a replica restaurant at their company headquarters. They used it during classroom training exercises to create experiential simulations. It was as close as they could get to the real world, without it being real.

Today, we can use virtual reality and other immersive technologies to provide realistic simulations for learning. You'll hear a lot more about these in later chapters.

Facilitator

The root of the word *facilitator* is *facile*, which is Latin for "make easy." The essence of being a facilitator is to make things easy for others.

Facilitators show up in many contexts. For example:

- **A marriage counselor** who steps in to help a couple work through conflict
- **A mediator** who helps two opposing interests negotiate a truce
- **A mentor/coach** who helps you incrementally improve

In each case, the recipient of the coaching, mediation, or counseling did the actual work; the facilitator was just there to enable and support it.

Meeting facilitators are also commonly used in workplace settings to help a group work through a process. For example, an executive team may bring in a meeting facilitator to help them craft a new business strategy. Or an organization in transition may use an external facilitator to help them make weighty decisions about their future. The facilitator isn't an active decision maker; instead, they help the group discuss and make decisions.

When it comes to learning, the same principles apply. Facilitators enable and support the learning process. They help prepare participants, guide them along a learning path, ask questions so they discover new meanings, and supplement with resources along the way. Facilitators debrief simulations and learning exercises and may even coordinate logistics or manage related technology tools.

Best practices for the general process of facilitation are widely documented. These techniques include managing tasks and processes, establishing group norms, encouraging discussion, asking questions to create meaningful dialogue, summarizing key points, and staying on track. Facilitation is one of the 23 capabilities in ATD's Talent Development Capability Model, which describes the facilitator role as a "catalyst for learning," with participants assuming "responsibility for their own learning" (ATD 2020b).

Putting It All Together

So, while the terms *learning*, *experience*, and *facilitator* in isolation have meaning and value, when combined to form the new role of learning experience facilitator, they take on a whole new meaning:

A learning experience facilitator guides participants along a journey of self-directed discovery, leading to learning results and tangible outcomes. They help create and shape a positive learning environment. They coach learners by asking pointed questions and sharing meaningful observations that lead to new insights. They help learners create connections between existing knowledge and new information. They foster relationships between like-minded learners who are on similar learning paths. And they encourage, nurture, and steer the learners toward the end goal of performance improvement. Learning experience facilitators encourage learning in all types of environments, including immersive ones.

Transitioning From Instructor or Trainer to Learning Experience Facilitator

You may still be wondering, what about the instructor role? As I mentioned earlier, there is still a time and place for presentations and teaching. The challenge to overcome is when facilitation is needed but instruction is provided.

Most people are familiar with the type of instruction practiced in formal education, such as grade school or college, where information is shared through lectures and readings to build the learner's general knowledge. This type of background knowledge may be a prerequisite to developing specialized skills. For example, a history major goes on to law school to become an attorney. Or a biology major graduates and goes on to pursue more education in a veterinary school.

However, general education as taught in schools and universities has a different goal from that of learning in the workplace. Talent development programs, the central underlying theme of this book, focus on *applied* knowledge and skills. Performance improvement is the goal. And when we update our methods of improving performance, we should also update our methods for getting it.

Instruction makes sense for novices who are learning new skills. Beginners need to start somewhere to gain context before diving into the deep end of exploration. However, the instructional methods that are most effective for novices are different from those that work for experienced individuals. Many beginners benefit from direct instruction as opposed to self-discovery (Clark 2020). In a workplace setting, beginners may learn these basics on the job or through a mixture of formal and informal training classes.

For example, if a brand-new software system rolls out in an organization, replacing an antiquated paper-based system, then people will need specific instructions to use the new system. Or in the case of new-hire orientation, the purpose is to familiarize new hires with expectations and acclimate them to organizational culture. In these and several other similar instances, it makes sense to include formal instruction in the training curriculum.

Some of this instruction could be provided as asynchronous self-led learning without trainer involvement, such as a job aid, videos, or other performance support materials. It's even possible that an organization could waste resources on formal instruction when it's not needed.

There is also value in hearing a subject matter expert (SME) present short bursts of content—for example, as a keynote speech, a conference presentation, or even a podcast. But this shouldn't be the only element of learning content. Think of it this way: You wouldn't want a driver to get behind the wheel of a car if they had only watched a video series featuring driving experts. Absorbing information from a presentation alone is valuable only when knowledge, not application, is the end goal. For application, you need relevant immersion.

VOICES FROM THE FIELD

"I started as an educator, then became a trainer and speaker, and now am a facilitator because I've realized that's where the learning happens. Facilitation means more work up front as we create engaging ways (that don't involve us!) for learners to interact with the material. You spend your time as a facilitator setting up and debriefing activities, so the learners do the work. They also do the learning."
—**Christie Ward, Principal, The Impact Institute**

What's in a Name?

The titles *trainer, instructor, educator,* and *facilitator* are often used inter-changeably in our industry. *Instructor* typically refers to a teaching role, someone who is an expert in the subject matter. *Educator* is often used in a formal educational setting, like a university. In some cases, educators are collectively referred to as *faculty*. *Trainer* is most commonly used in a work-place setting, referring to someone who delivers training programs for an organization's learning and development department. *Facilitator* can be a meeting facilitator, or a classroom facilitator.

For the purposes of this book, *facilitator* is our preferred title for a person who guides immersive, virtual, blended, and hybrid learning ex-periences. Regardless of which title your organization uses, I recommend adopting a facilitator mindset. You can act like a facilitator without actually being called one.

Skills of a Learning Experience Facilitator

The rest of this book will take a closer look at the facilitation skills needed in several different types of learning environments, including the immersive, virtual, blended, and hybrid classrooms. I'll address many skills ranging from active listening to the art of asking questions to managing group dy-namics, all in the context of immersive learning.

For now, Table 1-1 provides a brief comparison of traditional trainer skills and the skills needed from a learning experience facilitator. Note that some are exactly the same, while others represent an evolution.

Where to Begin

If you have any background in teaching or training, then rest assured you are not starting from scratch. It's like if you already know how to drive a car and you need to learn how to drive a bus—the basics are the same. As

TABLE 1-1. Traditional Trainer Skills vs. Learning Experience Facilitator Skills

Traditional Trainer	Learning Experience Facilitator
Presentation skills	Communication skills
Discussion leader	Discussion prompter
Storytelling from the stage	Storytelling in context
Flexibility	Improvisation
Encourage	Empathize
Research the audience	Relate to the audience
Ask direct questions	Ask discussion questions
Create connections between participant and content	Create connections among participants for learning
Process and debrief training activities	Process and debrief learning experiences
Activity planner	Engagement coordinator
Provide feedback	Provide feedback
Coach	Coach

a classroom trainer, you received a facilitator guide, studied the notes, got your classroom set up, and began the workshop.

As a skilled traditional trainer, you've probably already mastered the art of storytelling, learned how to capture an audience's attention, and honed your presentation skills. These tasks will help you become a better facilitator because elements of them are found in the facilitator's skill set.

My own journey from instructor to facilitator had a pivotal aha moment when I was still a fairly new trainer. After observing one of my half-day leadership workshops, my supervisor said, "Why don't you try sitting down during the group discussion time? You don't have to stand for the entire workshop." As simple as this advice sounds, it was a turning point for me. I realized that I could sit and discuss points *with* my learners instead of just feeling like I had to stay separated and teach the entire time. I could release control of the conversation, stepping in to steer and guide the participants only when needed.

What's Next

Because technology-enabled learning has paved the way for this new learning experience facilitator role, our next step is reviewing some technology terms. If you're already comfortable with the hardware and software of virtual learning technologies, including virtual and augmented reality, then feel free to skip over chapter 2. Otherwise, keep reading.

CHAPTER 2

Technology for Immersive Learning

When I was writing my first book on virtual training in the mid-2000s, I interviewed several trainers who had already embraced online delivery and asked them all the same question: *What is the number one piece of advice you would give to a new virtual facilitator?* I got the same response over and over: Learn the technology.

Since that time, I've worked with thousands of classroom trainers in their quests to become online facilitators, and I still fully agree with that advice. The best facilitators are ones who thoroughly know and understand the technology they use. This knowledge gives them more energy to expend on facilitation as opposed to having to waste time figuring out what button to press and when. They have an easier relationship with the equipment, which translates to a better facilitation flow. Furthermore, the more comfortable a facilitator is with the technology, the more seamless the experience is for learners.

You've seen this in action if you've ever participated in a virtual training workshop where the facilitator seems unfamiliar or unprepared. They could be frustrated that their video isn't working correctly. Or they may say something like "I think you're supposed to click on top" when you're actually supposed to click on the bottom. Or they might stumble over their words because they are struggling with something behind the scenes. Of course, there are several possible reasons for these facilitation mistakes, but one likely cause is a lack of comfort with the platform tools.

In today's technology-saturated world, you might think that everyone is tech-savvy. Yet that assumption couldn't be further from the truth. Not everyone uses computers on a regular basis, and not everyone keeps up with the latest innovations. This is particularly true with immersive, blended, and hybrid learning.

It was not that many years ago when I needed to teach my workshop participants how to use a mouse. More than once, I watched someone pick it up to wave it in the air or let it travel down the side of their desk to try to position their onscreen cursor. And I still have to teach some attendees of my virtual training classes how to use basic controls like raise hand and mute. Just like most people now know how to use a mouse or trackpad, eventually most people will know how a virtual platform's commands work. And one day, the same will be true for immersive technologies like VR hand controllers and AR apps. But until then, it's important to teach the fundamentals.

I mention this because some of the concepts and explanations in this chapter may seem quite basic to you. But remember that not everyone has the same level of comfort with technology, and I want us to all be on the same page as we move through this content. So, I'm going to err on the side of caution and include a lot of definitions. I'd rather provide too much than not enough and leave someone wondering. Think of this chapter as a simple primer on learning technologies for learning experience facilitators in immersive, virtual, blended, and hybrid contexts.

VOICES FROM THE FIELD

"What helps me learn a new technology is to get a test account and play in it. I set up test meetings with friends and then just "learn on the fly." I also search the web for how-to videos, and review the vendor support pages. These are great resources to use." **—Marion Schilcher, business coach, trainer, and facilitator**

Overview of Technology Used in Immersive Learning Environments

At its most basic level, and for the purposes of this book, *technology* is a set of tools used by designers, facilitators, and learners to create learning experiences. It's most often identified as hardware—tangible items like devices, headsets, cameras, and wearables—that can be touched and used. But it also encompasses software—which is intangible but still very real.

The technology terms that follow are organized in a logical progression starting with big picture concepts, then narrowing down into specific topics and corresponding accompaniments. Let's start with two overarching concepts to set the stage, then dive into the specifics of hybrid, blended, and immersive learning tech.

Asynchronous vs. Synchronous

Asynchronous learning events are self-led or self-directed activities that participants complete on their own, without a designated start and stop time. Examples include watching a video, reading a book, or taking an online e-learning course. *Synchronous events* involve participants meeting together at the same time with a facilitator; this can happen either online or in person. Most modern learning experiences include a combination of synchronous and asynchronous events.

Virtual Classroom (or Virtual Training)

When a facilitator and learners come together for a synchronous event, but are not physically in the same location, the environment they're in is commonly called the virtual classroom. Some also refer to this as "virtual training" or even the "live online classroom." My long-time definition of virtual training is:

> A highly interactive, synchronous online, instructor-led training class, with defined learning objectives, that has geographically dispersed participants, each one individually connected using a web classroom platform. (Huggett 2014)

Notice the key words in this definition:

- **Highly interactive:** Participants engage frequently, at least every few minutes, with the facilitator, with the learning content, and with the virtual classroom tools.
- **Synchronous online:** Participants meet at the same time. Sometimes referred to as "live" or, in the case of virtual training, "live online."
- **Instructor-led:** Facilitated by a professional trainer or facilitator.
- **Defined learning objectives:** Clearly stated performance expectations that learners will be able to achieve as a result of actively participating in the session.
- **Geographically dispersed:** Participants are distributed and apart from one another, not in the same room.
- **Individually connected:** Each participant joins from their own device and has their own audio connection.
- **Web classroom platform:** The "training" or "classroom" version of a software program that allows for online screen and file sharing, as well as robust audience interaction tools such as polling, whiteboarding, and breakouts.

A fundamental premise of the virtual classroom is that it's different from an online meeting, a videoconference, a webcast, or a webinar. In fact, each type of online event has a different goal and expected outcome. Meetings and videoconferences are usually used for status updates and action items. Webcasts and webinars are typically one-way presentations. But a virtual training class is used to bring about performance outcomes and behavior change by focusing on dialogue, discussion, and collaboration (Figure 2-1).

A typical virtual training class has fewer than 25 participants and is scheduled for 60-to-90-minute chunks of time (Huggett 2021). Several virtual classes are often strung together in a series to create a complete curriculum.

FIGURE 2-1. An Example Virtual Class in Action

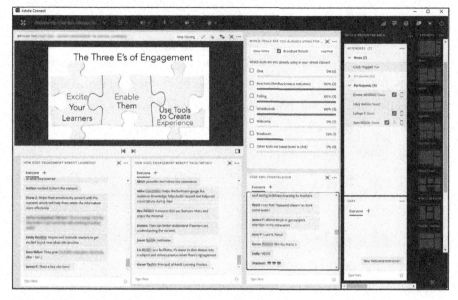

Adobe product screenshot reprinted with permission from Adobe Inc.

However, for the purposes of this book, the most important thing to know about the virtual classroom is that the traditional virtual classroom—although still alive and well—is being replaced by the modern virtual classroom. Chapter 3 provides a detailed look at the transition, and how to facilitate for engagement.

By the way, don't confuse *virtual classroom* or *virtual training* with *virtual reality*—we'll get to that later in the chapter.

Hybrid Classroom

When some learners are together in the same location, and other learners are remote, it's a hybrid class. Hybrid classes have risen in popularity mainly due to the COVID-19 pandemic. Following the lockdowns of 2020, some organizations that reopened their offices also decided to retain their remote work policies. Therefore, many facilitators will need to accommodate both in-person and remote audiences in their training classes.

Note that in some contexts, especially higher education, a hybrid class means a combination of asynchronous and synchronous activities. However, in workplace learning environments, that type of learning experience is called blended learning or a "learning journey" (as discussed in the next section). In this book, we'll use the more common definition of *hybrid classes*: a mixed-audience learning experience. Chapter 4 provides a complete how-to guide for facilitating hybrid classes.

Blended Learning

When synchronous and asynchronous components are intentionally combined to create a complete training curriculum, it's called blended learning. The experience is structured from start to finish, and often completed in groups of participants, called a cohort.

For example, I recently needed to renew my basic life support certification (more commonly known as CPR). When I signed up for the course I received access to an online learning portal, through which I completed several self-led e-learning modules with a test at the end of each one. After completing those requirements, I attended the in-person classroom component. While in the in-person program we practiced the hands-on skills, and I was able to ask questions of the facilitator and demonstrate my new expertise. This combination of synchronous and asynchronous events totaled the complete blended learning program.

The concept of blended learning isn't new, but it is known by several different names. So, when you hear someone say they are designing a "guided learning journey" or putting together a "learning campaign" or creating a "learning series," it's safe to assume they mean blended learning.

Remember, chapter 5 is all about facilitator skills in blended learning journeys. We'll take a closer look at the facilitator role and the skills needed for success in that environment.

Learning Platforms

Most blended learning journeys are hosted in a *learning platform*. This online environment provides a home base for participants going through a multicomponent curriculum, telling them what task to complete, when to complete it, and where to access the assignments.

Learning platforms generally refer to an online software system with database functionality. You can think of a learning platform like a well-organized virtual file cabinet. But it is more than just a simple electronic database—the learning platform hosts, tracks, manages, compiles, combines, and more. There are a few different types of learning platforms you may encounter as a facilitator; let's take a brief look at each.

Learning Management System

A learning management system (LMS) could be considered the original learning platform. It's a database that serves as a repository for learning materials. Instructional designers can create course components to load into an LMS, which in turn lets learners access them. Many LMSs have discussion boards, quizzes, and other simple built-in interactions.

A training curriculum stored in an LMS is usually linear. It has a set starting point and set finishing point, with a prescribed learning path to take. The hallmark of an LMS is that it can track a participant's course progress, storing test scores, completion rates, time spent, and other analytics. Its middle name, *management*, explains it well—it's an administrative tool used to manage learning activities.

Learning management systems, while still available and in use by many organizations, have largely lost favor in comparison to learning experience platforms.

Learning Experience Platform

The learning experience platform (LXP) is the next step forward from an LMS. Instead of focusing only on the back-end database, an LXP also emphasizes the front-end learner experience. It allows learners to interact with a variety of learning components in many ways. LXPs still include administrative reporting and tracking functions—using analytics to measure progress and learning—but their appeal is the user experience.

A key differentiator between an LMS and an LXP is that the learner can take more control in an LXP. This is possible because the LXP curates information, allows user-generated content sharing, and provides options for social collaboration. LXPs give each learner a personalized experience, similar to popular video-streaming services that recommend what to watch next (Figure 2-2).

FIGURE 2-2. Example of an LXP Platform, Intrepid

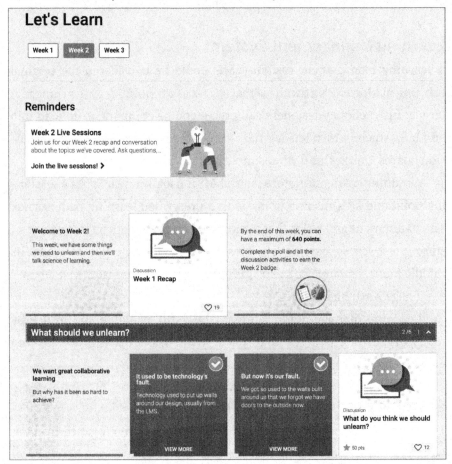

Intrepid screenshot reprinted with permission from Intrepid.

Virtual Classroom Platforms

While on the subject of platforms, let's also consider virtual classroom platforms. To be clear, these are very different from the LMS and LXP we've just discussed. They're web-based videoconferencing software systems that allow learners to meet with a facilitator in an online classroom. I have always referred to this type of software as a *virtual classroom platform*.

Not every web-based videoconferencing software program is designed for hosting virtual classes. Many are simply online meeting platforms. Some vendors in the virtual meeting space offer a suite of products for different types of online events, such as one product for meetings and a separate product for webinars. Each product has a different set of features and a different target audience.

The virtual classroom platform market is in rapid transformation. There has been lightning-fast development since the COVID-19 pandemic led many organizations to shift to online learning in early 2020. Every major product vendor has released product updates. In addition, vendors are consolidating features from among different products to meet demands for simplicity. For example, breakout rooms—once the distinguishing factor of the virtual classroom platform—can now be found in most meeting platforms.

These platforms come with a variety of tools that we'll explore in the next chapter. But first, let's discuss some of the platforms and technology that are specific to virtual, augmented, and mixed reality.

Virtual Reality

If you were to ask 100 people for the definition of a virtual classroom, a few would respond by saying virtual reality (VR). Yet the similarity pretty much ends with the fact that they both begin with the word *virtual*.

Merriam-Webster defines *virtual* as "being such in essence or effect though not formally recognized or admitted." From this, we can infer that *virtual reality* means "almost reality" or "nearly reality." It's the essence of reality, in a computer-simulated environment.

Imagine you are watching a scene from *Star Trek* and the ship's crew wants to visit a faraway location—for relaxation, entertainment, or study—but they don't want to travel there. So instead they go to the ship's Holodeck, program in the experience, and enter an exact replica of it. They can interact with characters, pick up objects, and be immersed in the space. Then, with just one computer command, everything disappears and they're just sitting in an empty room on the spaceship. The journey seemed real, but it wasn't (Figure 2-3).

FIGURE 2-3. Example VR Learning Experience in Action

Immerse screenshot reprinted with permission from Immerse (immerse.online)

This type of immersive yet contrived experience aptly describes virtual reality. It is fully artificial yet seems fully real. (Of course, this assumes it's a well-designed virtual reality environment. We'll talk about *fidelity*, *immersion*, and *presence* later.)

In lieu of *Star Trek*'s massive spaceships, most people today use special hardware that is worn on the body, enabling us to experience a truly virtual environment. These items take over our senses: goggles for our seeing eyes, controllers for our feeling hands, and earbuds for our hearing ears. Some systems even offer haptic feedback through sensors in shoes and bodysuits. And while not yet readily available, sensors for taste and smell are under active research and someday will be part of the standard gear (Matchar 2018, Lefrak 2022). By putting on this VR equipment, it's possible to become truly immersed in a virtual world.

Here are several VR terms that facilitators should be familiar with:

- **Field of view (FoV):** The FoV is everything you can see inside a headset display. It's how much of the virtual environment you can see at any given time.

- **Degrees of freedom:** The amount of movement that's tracked increases with the number of degrees of freedom you have when wearing a VR headset. Three degrees of freedom (3DoF) and six degrees of freedom (6DoF) are the two most common. 3DOF tracks your head movement (pitch, yaw, and roll, which means up/down, left/right, and roll); 6DoF tracks your location or position in the physical space in addition to your head movement. In other words, in 3DoF VR, you can look around; in 6DoF VR, you can move around.

- **Fidelity:** The realistic quality of a virtual reality environment is known as its fidelity. The higher the screen resolution, the more realistic the experience feels.

- **Immersion:** Immersion is determined by how closely a virtual environment mirrors a real one. For example, viewing a 2-D drawing of a building is less immersive than standing inside the building. It might help to think about how immersion can happen outside the VR environment, such as when you lose track of time while reading a really good book or become fully engaged in a realistic role play with another participant.

- **Presence:** The degree to which someone is fully engrossed in the virtual reality environment is reflected in its presence. While often intertwined with the term *immersion*, presence is different—it's when a situation evokes a response from you. For example, if you've ever cried while watching a movie or if a book character's poor decisions have made you feel anxious, you've experienced presence.

▸ **360-degree video:** Fully immersive videos are considered a form of virtual reality because they can pull you inside the photographed scene. Traditional videos, like the kind created with a video camera or smartphone, have a limited field of view that captures only the scene in front of the lens. A 360-degree video, on the other hand, captures the surrounding environment—not just what's in front, but also what's behind and on either side. Some VR scenarios are created using this type of immersive media, whether using panoramic photos stitched together or 360-degree video clips.

Now, let's take a closer look at the gear that makes these VR concepts possible.

Headsets

Also known as a *head mounted display* (or *HMD* for short), VR headsets are often called goggles, although they don't quite look like your traditional swim goggles or even the eye protection goggles used in a science lab. VR goggles are a computer device that is affixed to your head and covers your eyes.

The headset has a display screen that is placed inside the frame, with panels that block your view of the surrounding world. Screen quality varies, with higher resolutions resulting in better quality. In a VR headset, increased sharpness and better resolution make for a better virtual experience.

Two types of VR headsets are typically used for learning events:

▸ **Tethered headsets** are connected by a wire to a high-powered computer. While the wire limits movement, it allows the computing power to stay in the computer, which usually results in a less bulky headset.

▸ **Stand-alone headsets** either use Bluetooth technology to connect to a computer or contain enough computing power to independently run VR applications. Because the headset is not wired to anything else, the user can move freely. Stand-alone headsets have become more accessible and affordable in recent years, and are the hardware of choice for most immersive learning experiences.

Keep in mind that VR headsets are more than just simple display screens. When wearing a VR headset with motion tracking, you'll see the ceiling of the virtual room if you look up. When you look left or right, you'll see each side. And when you walk, your perception will change as if you are walking inside the virtual room. This change of view is possible because of the headset's motion-tracking technology.

The motion tracking may be done through external sensors that detect movement or miniature cameras that capture input. Newer headsets can even use magnetic fields or ultrasound waves to gather data. These sensory signals then send information to the software, which in turn changes what you view on the screen. The better the motion tracker, the better the virtual reality experience.

Controllers

Some VR technology uses handheld controllers to enhance motion tracking and the virtual experience. If you've ever used a TV remote, or played a video game that uses a joystick, then you are familiar with the fundamental concept. Controllers are input devices that help you manipulate what's happening on the screen.

VR controllers allow for communication between the physical world and the digital one. For example, in a VR environment, you can point a controller at a door and click on it to open it, or you can use it to select a character to interact with.

Not all VR experiences use hand controllers, but most do. Many vendors are adopting hand-gesture-recognition technology that replaces the need for controllers. This allows you to use your hands to point, pinch, or grab and interact with digital objects.

Web-Based Virtual Reality

With all this discussion about hardware and equipment, you might think that VR requires a full garment of learning technologies to fully realize its potential. And many organizations have avoided or delayed adopting VR solutions because the equipment seems expensive and wearing it can feel bulky and uncomfortable.

But innovation and ingenuity have expanded VR to the computer screen. Instead of putting on a headset, the learner can simply open their browser to see the virtual environment and interact with it. While this type of web-based VR is not considered immersive virtual reality, it can still provide a simulation experience. For example, many computer-based video games are examples of web-based VR—they immerse you into the story line, add sound effects, and provide realistic scenarios.

Web-based virtual reality can be a gateway for cash-strapped or cost-conservative organizations looking to enter the digital simulation world.

As we conclude this overview of VR equipment and terms, perhaps the most important thing to remember is how rapidly these devices are changing. Updates, enhancements, and new releases are happening all the time, and the more the devices change, the more accessible they will become.

We'll explore facilitator skills for VR in chapter 7.

WHAT ABOUT THE METAVERSE?

It's nearly impossible to talk about virtual reality without acknowledging the newest buzzword: *metaverse*. While there is debate over its exact definition, most would agree that the metaverse is an immersive virtual world with many engaging components. It's a collection of virtual spaces that some envision as a new digital universe where people—in avatar form—can both work and play. Think of it like a virtual all-inclusive vacation resort, with a business center for working, restaurants for eating, a marketplace for shopping, daytime activities for entertainment, and nightlife for socializing. With all these immersive virtual spaces, it's hard to imagine that learning experiences won't one day be part of the metaverse. However, this book doesn't focus on the metaverse as a whole, except to acknowledge that, like the internet is to virtual training, one day the metaverse may be to immersive learning.

Augmented Reality

You have probably encountered augmented reality (AR) as a consumer. It's become prolific in all types of media, especially social media. For example, if you've seen a boundary line superimposed on the field while watching sports on TV, you've seen augmented reality. Or if you've taken a selfie and added playful elements like dog ears before sharing it with friends, you've used augmented reality (Figure 2-4).

FIGURE 2-4. Selfie With AR

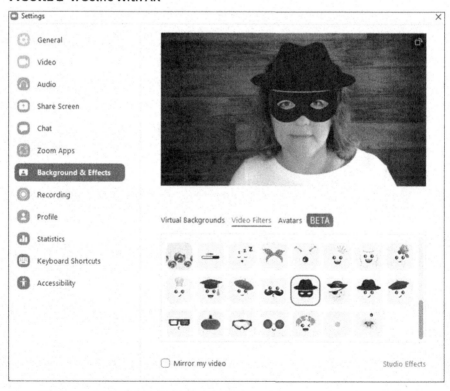

©Zoom Video Communications, Inc. Reprinted with permission.

Augmented reality is exactly what its name implies: the real world with digital elements added to it. When you experience AR, you still see the real world, with digital enhancements. Sometimes the digital elements are obvious, while other times they are seamlessly integrated.

AR and VR share some similarities, but they create quite different experiences. The biggest difference is that AR digital content doesn't actually interact with the real world; it simply sits on top of it. In other words, the digital world adds to or enhances the real one.

For example, if you are shopping for furniture online and want to visualize how a chair would look in your living room before you actually purchase it, you can use augmented reality to superimpose the chair on your space. Or, if you are traveling overseas and are trying to read a restaurant menu, you could use augmented reality to translate those words into your native language. Or, if you aren't sure how to use a new coffee maker, you could open the electronic manual on your smartphone and see pop-up instructions to help you brew a cup.

There are countless examples of how augmented reality enhances the world around us, and so many opportunities to use it for just-in-time learning. But before we discuss how facilitators can use it for learning applications (that's in chapter 6!), let's back up and learn more about it.

AR Equipment

Most AR requires some type of equipment to help you see and experience it. The most common tool is the camera in a mobile device. Some AR programs also require a specialized app that's downloaded onto your smartphone or tablet, which in turn uses its built-in camera.

AR can also be viewed through a headset or glasses equipped with built-in specialty lenses. These headsets differ from those used for VR, because the lenses are clear and don't block your view of what's going on around you.

The original AR headset, Google Glass, was a pair of glasses with computing capability. More recently, Snapchat released sunglasses, called Spectacles, that have built-in cameras designed for AR experiences. Other AR accessories include smartwatches and rings. Because these items are worn on the body, they are collectively called "wearables." As technology evolves, expect to see an increase in the types and styles of wearable devices.

AR Concepts

In addition to the terminology already covered in the VR section, two other AR prevalent concepts to know are *anchor* and *marker*:

- **An anchor** is what connects an augmented digital object to the real world. Similar to a ship's anchor, which tethers it to a distinctive location, an AR anchor tells the AR program where to place and hold a digital object onscreen. The anchor helps the digital object stay in one place even if you move your camera lens to a different viewing area.

- **A marker** is an object in the real world—a photo, sign, or geographical coordinate—that triggers an AR experience. For example, you can open your smartphone camera and point it at an AR marker to start the AR experience. In addition, some virtual classroom platforms are now using hand gesture markers to display AR components on screen.

Note that while they may look very similar, QR codes are not exactly the same as AR markers. AR can be launched from a QR code, but not all QR codes are AR. QR codes are most often used to open websites—like a hot key on a keyboard. You can also use a QR code to launch an AR experience, overlaying digital content on your existing environment. See Figures 2-5 and 2-6 on the next page for an example of each type, featuring messages from me that demonstrate the two different formats. Use your smartphone camera to experience each one in action.

FIGURE 2-5. QR Code for a Video Message From Cindy

FIGURE 2-6. AR Marker Inviting Cindy's Avatar Into Your Workspace

We'll revisit these concepts, along with other features of augmented reality, in chapter 6.

Mixed Reality

Mixed reality (MR) means exactly what it sounds like—it's a mixture of VR, AR, and the real world. This space allows digital content to interact with the real world around you. MR is more immersive than AR, but not quite as immersive as VR. It often includes the use of 3-D objects. The *Downton Abbey* exhibit described in the introduction of this book was an MR experience because it incorporated a mixture of these digital elements in a physical location.

In a mixed reality experience, you might be in a meeting room, looking at a conference table with holographic images around it. You can interact with these digital images, moving them around or changing their behavior. At the time of this writing, the most widely known use of mixed reality is in Microsoft's proprietary HoloLens glasses.

Extended Reality

Extended reality (XR) is an overarching term that encompasses VR, AR, and MR. It's often used when referring to immersive technologies as a whole. For example, an instructional designer who specializes in developing all types of immersive learning may simply say that they design XR experiences. Even though it isn't necessarily a separate concept from VR, AR, and MR, it's worth recognizing the name and being aware of its meaning.

Comparing VR, AR, and MR

To summarize the key differences between VR, AR, and MR, think of it this way (Figure 2-7):

- **VR** completely immerses you in a digital environment.
- **AR** overlays digital objects on the real world. It's the real world, enriched with digital objects.
- **MR** combines the real world and virtual content. It allows digital objects to interact with the real world.

FIGURE 2-7. Comparing VR, AR, and MR

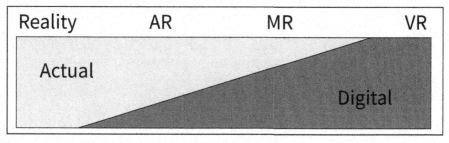

In Summary

Now that you are familiar with the fundamental learning technologies used by learning experience facilitators, we can put this knowledge to use. We'll start with the virtual classroom.

Checklist: Ways to Learn Technology

To help you get comfortable with the tech tools and concepts that you'll use in learning experiences, consider the following activities:

- [ ] Sign up for online classes available from the vendor, or on curated sites like LinkedIn Learning.
- [ ] Watch tutorials on the vendor's video channel.
- [ ] Read all of the available help and support screens.
- [ ] Attend vendor sessions as a participant.
- [ ] Subscribe to the vendor's newsletters.
- [ ] Purchase the tool (or a demo copy of it) and practice using it.
- [ ] Click on every button—try it!
- [ ] Participate in user discussions (find groups on social media to match the platform or tool).

CHAPTER 3

Facilitating Immersive Virtual Classes

Virtual classrooms have been around for more than 20 years, and they are here to stay. Use of virtual classrooms for formal training slowly grew from 5 percent in 2000, to 10 percent in 2005, and to 14 percent in 2019 (ATD 2020a). In 2020, that number skyrocketed due to the worldwide COVID-19 pandemic, with many organizations quickly switching much of their training from in-person to online. ATD reported that 98 percent of the organizations surveyed in 2021 used virtual classrooms, and nine in 10 of those organizations cited the pandemic as a major driver (ATD 2021).

Despite the increased adoption of virtual training over time, it has not necessarily been a smooth ride because many see virtual as a lesser option when compared with in-person classes. There are numerous reasons for this—some are simply incorrect perceptions, but others are a valid reflection of the truth. Unfortunately, many unskilled facilitators are prone to blandly lecturing at remote audiences, and classes can be hindered by lack of engaging design.

Thankfully, designers who embrace interactivity and facilitators who are able to engage remote audiences have found success with participants who learn new skills and apply them on the job. Virtual training *can* be extremely effective when it's well designed and effectively facilitated.

Today, the old-fashioned "listen while someone presents content" model of virtual training is no longer relevant or even tolerated. Participants can (and will) easily check out and do other things unless they are actively participating in a virtual class. It takes a capable facilitator with a *current mindset*, an *updated tool set*, and a *relevant skill set* to effectively deliver immersive learning experiences. This is true in each new environment addressed in this book, and especially virtual classes. So let's take a deeper dive into each one—the mindset, tool set, and skill set—starting with mindset.

FIGURE 3-1. Hallmarks of a Learning Experience Facilitator

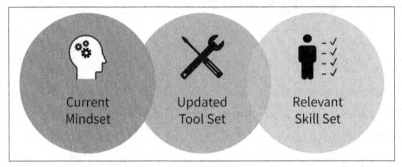

A Current Mindset: Presenting vs. Facilitating

Remember, my longtime definition of virtual training is:

> A highly interactive online synchronous facilitator-led class, which has defined learning objectives, with participants who are connected individually from geographically dispersed locations, using a web-based virtual classroom platform.

I've shared this definition with thousands of people during conference sessions, webcasts, and seminars. My follow-up question is then, "What stands out to you in this definition?" Nearly everyone says "Highly interactive," as if that's an unusual perspective to have. Many people just assume that if the session is online, it will be a more passive experience than if it was in person.

In fact, 15 percent of respondents to my State of Virtual Training 2022 survey selected "presentation with one or more speakers" as their definition of virtual training (Huggett 2021). That's a significant number of training professionals who equate learning with lectures.

I get it. It's easy to confuse online presentations with virtual training classes. They are both live online events. They both use web-conferencing platforms. They both have presenters and distributed audiences. However, as much as they seem alike, they have very different purposes and outcomes. Virtual presentations—often called webcasts or webinars—provide information to the masses. They are usually recorded for playback and involve one-way communication. Virtual classes, on the other hand, have learning objectives and measurable results. They allow discussion, collaboration, and opportunities to practice new skills while receiving feedback. And they can be immersive.

Sometimes organizations need to implement a training solution quickly and don't have the time to adequately repurpose training content for the virtual classroom. Or they need to quickly scale a solution, so they invite too many people to the online events. I've also talked with many virtual trainers who want to interact with their remote audiences, but ultimately resort to presenting because they aren't sure if participants are paying attention.

While lectures may have a place in a curriculum, they do not get the same results as interactive, immersive learning. Think of it this way: Do you want to be operated on by a doctor who simply listened to lectures on how to perform the procedure? Of course not! Having just enough knowledge may sometimes be OK, but it's not enough for most situations. It's vital to recognize the difference.

That's why the mindset shift from presenting to facilitating is so important. To be a highly rated virtual presenter, you must have interesting content and good storytelling techniques. To be a learning experience facilitator in the virtual classroom, you must add more. It takes determination, effort, and a specialized skill set to keep the spotlight on the remote audience and their learning outcomes.

This new mindset means transferring the focus from the words you say to the words participants say. From speaking at the screen to speaking with the people on the other side of the screen. From looking at your presentation notes to looking at the participants' responses. From emphasizing yourself as speaker to highlighting the audience as active participants.

Let's review three techniques to help you shift your mindset to one of a learning experience facilitator:

- **Listen to your vocabulary.** What words do you use when describing virtual training classes? Do you call them "presentations"? Do you refer to your role as a "teacher," "speaker," or "presenter"? Do you call the facilitator guide your "script" or your "speaker notes"? While your word choices may not seem important, they may indicate your underlying thoughts and influence your behavior. Start by changing your words.
- **Ask yourself, "Who's doing the most talking?"** If you aren't sure, use a tool like Riff Analytics to measure the conversation dynamics, or ask a trusted colleague to observe your session. If the scale is tipped in your direction instead of the participants', you've likely slipped into presentation mode. Go through the program to consciously determine where you could reduce your talking to shift from presenter to facilitator.
- **Consider the participant viewpoint.** If the participants' learning experience is largely the same whether they've attended live or watched a recorded playback, then they likely weren't involved in the learning and it was probably a presentation. Use this litmus test to help you determine if you should provide an asynchronous experience instead. If a recording would suffice, then respect your adult audience enough to provide one instead of forcing them to show up at a designated time.

It takes time and effort to rewire your thinking and find a new paradigm. Fortunately, the modern virtual classroom is full of collaboration tools that support this effort. Let's turn there now.

An Updated Tool Set: Modern Virtual Classrooms

The collaborative tools found in today's modern virtual classrooms have their foundation in legacy platforms. Some, like chat and polling, have been part of virtual classes for many years. Many have evolved over time with updated features or new use applications. Let's look at the traditional virtual classroom first.

Hallmarks of the traditional virtual classroom include three things:

- **Authority of the virtual trainer.** Many traditional virtual trainers use the platform tools to dominate the conversation. They may be the only person with their camera on, they may take up most of the mic time, and they may moderate participant interaction with a heavy hand. This tends to push programs into presentation mode.
- **Ability to internally share files inside the virtual classroom.** While two methods have almost always existed for sharing content with remote participants—file upload and screenshare—traditional virtual classrooms leaned heavily on showing slides on the main screen, which can easily shift a learning event into a presentation. When a slide deck is the focal point throughout a virtual class, many participants remain passive observers.
- **Activities that allow for participant involvement.** Standard tools like polling, chatting, whiteboarding, feedback indicators, and breakout rooms have always been part of virtual classrooms. The more creatively a virtual trainer used these features, the more engaging the virtual class tended to be. And while these collaboration tools were sometimes used for involvement and engagement, the current technology can make them really shine.

So, what sets apart the modern virtual classroom from these original features? Let's explore that next.

Traditional vs. Modern Classroom Tools

Modern virtual classrooms are fresh and interesting, and can be downright fun. They have remnants of traditional virtual classes while standing solidly in the modern digital era. They are noted by two distinguishing factors:

- A virtual classroom platform created and used for collaboration
- An immersive participant experience full of meaningful and relevant engagement that leads to learning and application

TABLE 3-1. Traditional vs. Modern Virtual Classroom Platform Tools

Traditional Tool	Modern Tool	What's New?
Internal document sharing	Screen sharing	The flexibility afforded by real-time screen sharing
Chat	Enhanced chat	Ability to use graphics, emojis, and other visual communication methods
Annotate or draw	Enhanced drawing	From rigid rules about drawing on screen to more flexible features and functions
Whiteboard	Collaborative whiteboards	Better group brainstorming activities with more accessibility and tools
Raise hand	Hand-gesture recognition	From clicking on a simulated raise hand button to just raising your hand and having the system recognize your physical movement
Status indicators and nonverbal feedback	Emojis	More inclusive emotions and feelings are represented
Poll	Enhanced polling	Additional types of questions and responses now available (e.g., multiple choice, word clouds, and sliding scales)
Breakouts	Enhanced breakouts	Ability to choose your own room allows for greater participant control
Application or screen sharing	Enhanced screen sharing	More precise control of sharing creates a better and more seamless participant experience (e.g., virtual backgrounds and prerecorded media files)
Video	Enhanced video with AR features	Ability to use a video-first layout with augmented virtual backgrounds for content sharing

In the past, a virtual classroom platform might get a software update once a year or every other year. But when most of the world shifted to remote work in 2020, platform vendors dramatically accelerated feature development. Most updates are now occurring every month or even more frequently, bringing new and improved tools to the forefront. And many of these new features fall under the purview of the collaborative, modern classroom.

Today, virtual classroom platforms go beyond the simple video meeting by including features and functions that encourage *conversation, collaboration,* and *cooperation.*

These new virtual tools shift the balance from static to dynamic. From presentation to collaboration. From passive to active. And from trainer-focused to participant-focused. These changes are supported by the architecture of the platform tools.

Modern Virtual Classroom Tools

The evolution of virtual classroom tools has made it easier to collaborate. When used intentionally, these tools can enhance the learning experience by creating more opportunities for discussion and dialogue among participants. They allow for better communication, increased participant input, and more robust activities. Ultimately, they lead to better learning experiences, which lead to better learning transfer. Let's take a closer look at the popular new tools and their most common uses in the immersive virtual classroom.

Emoji Feedback

Virtual classrooms have had a "raise hand" feature for a very long time. Participants could click an icon to raise their hand or choose a status (such as "agree" or "disagree"). Today's virtual classrooms have taken these indicators to the next level thanks to the hundreds of emojis now available (Figure 3-2). The sheer number of possible expressions allows participants to show more diverse reactions. For example, it becomes possible to express confusion instead of disagreement, which have two different shades of meaning. In addition, many of the emoji options allow for personalization, such as the ability to change the emoji's skin tone.

In addition, AI-driven hand-gesture recognition is becoming more common. When enabled, a participant simply needs to clap their hands together to show applause or show a thumbs-up sign to indicate agreement. By removing the step of finding and clicking on an icon, these AI-driven tools allow participants to become more immersed in the virtual experience. The reactions appear automatically as participants talk with their hands, seamlessly adding a digital enhancement to the conversation.

FIGURE 3-2. Example of Emoji Feedback in Zoom

©Zoom Video Communications, Inc. Reprinted with permission.

Next-Gen Polling

Polls are a classic way to gather participant input during a virtual class. They can also be used as a knowledge check or quiz to determine understanding. A few legacy platforms even included short-answer questions, which allow for free-form text responses.

In today's modern virtual classrooms, polling options have expanded to include many types of questions and responses. Facilitators can post multiple-choice and short-answer polls, along with more complex polls that provide ratings, rankings, word clouds, matrices, and more. These features may be built into the platform, or they may be part of an extension that incorporates external polling software.

Facilitators can use these features to start a robust discussion on a certain topic or provide space for everyone—including otherwise quiet participants—to provide equal input. Polls are also a great way to gather participant feedback, which can then inform the next set of learning activities (Figure 3-3). With so many options for creative discussion starters, the possibilities are endless.

FIGURE 3-3. Example of Advanced Polling in Zoom

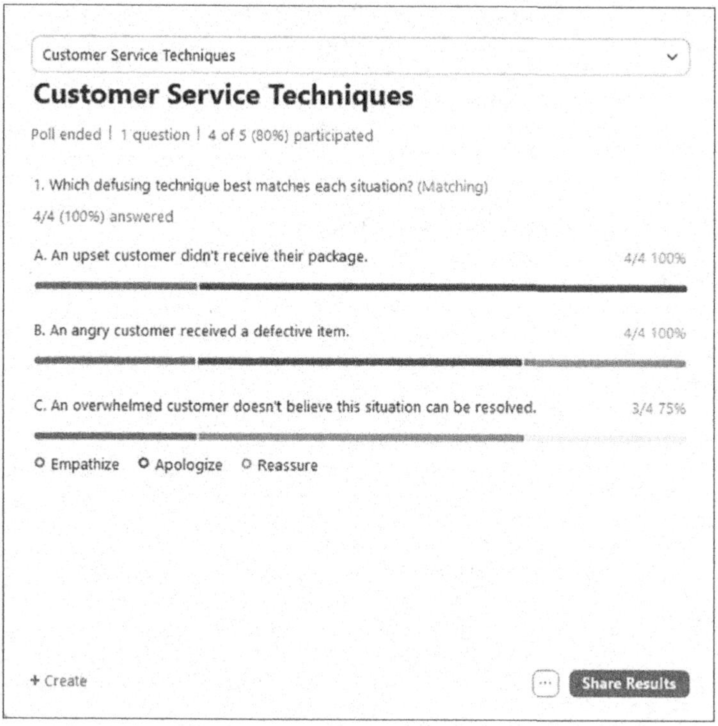

Customer Service Techniques

Customer Service Techniques

Poll ended | 1 question | 4 of 5 (80%) participated

1. Which defusing technique best matches each situation? (Matching)
4/4 (100%) answered

A. An upset customer didn't receive their package. — 4/4 100%

B. An angry customer received a defective item. — 4/4 100%

C. An overwhelmed customer doesn't believe this situation can be resolved. — 3/4 75%

O Empathize   O Apologize   O Reassure

+ Create   ···   Share Results

©Zoom Video Communications, Inc. Reprinted with permission.

Shared Whiteboards

A virtual whiteboard is like any physical whiteboard or blank chart paper you would find in a traditional classroom. In addition, the annotation (or drawing) tools in most virtual platforms can also be used on top of slides or shared screens.

Online drawing tools and whiteboards have always had a place in the virtual classroom. So, what's new? Modern virtual platforms provide enhanced drawing tools, the ability to overlay more sophisticated graphics, and a larger annotation space for working. You'll also find digital sticky notes and robust collaboration tools. Many external whiteboard software vendors even offer templates for use in predetermined activities.

For example, in a recent virtual training class, I divided participants into three teams. Each team went into a breakout room with instructions to brainstorm and record in a designated area on a shared whiteboard. What they didn't realize was that each team was simultaneously annotating different parts of the same large whiteboard. And, like a jigsaw puzzle, the four pieces came together when we returned to the main group and reviewed the whiteboard in its entirety (Figure 3-4).

FIGURE 3-4. Example of Shared Whiteboard in Zoom

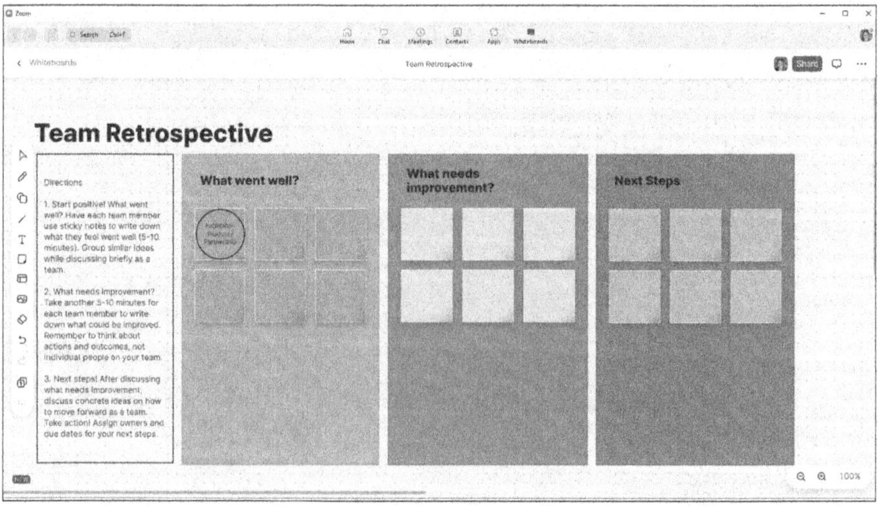

©Zoom Video Communications, Inc. Reprinted with permission.

Webcams

Two-thirds of the respondents to my annual State of Virtual Training in 2022 survey said they had increased their webcam use starting in 2020 (Huggett 2021). The overall increase in using webcams for remote work during the COVID-19 pandemic translated to a higher expectation of webcam use in the virtual classroom. I've seen it in my own virtual classes, and you probably have too.

Although use of video has been available in the virtual classroom for many years, it was not widely used. In fact, I advised against using them in my first book, *Virtual Training Basics*, which I wrote in 2009. Most people didn't have access to a webcam at the time, and if they did, they likely didn't have sufficient bandwidth to support it. However, when I updated the text in 2018 for the second edition, the very first thing I changed was the section on webcams. I encouraged their use then, and I still do today.

One reason for the increased usage is that most platforms are now video-first. In other words, the platform expects participants to connect their audio and video upon joining the online room. The first visible screen after clicking the connection link is usually an audio/video check—like an actor's greenroom—for you to test, adjust, and select the correct settings.

Another reason for the increased use is the wider availability of webcams in general. Almost all laptops and internet-connected devices now include a built-in webcam, which makes them easy to use.

Using webcams creates a sense of connection among remote attendees, provided that they are used with intention at the right times. For example, at the start of a virtual class, when everyone is meeting one another for the first time, webcams can help encourage relationships. If you've ever heard someone's voice on the phone and pictured them in your mind, only to someday discover that they look completely different than you imagined, then you know the power of both seeing and hearing another human while they are speaking.

Webcams also help create an immersive learning experience that goes beyond an audio-only conversation because it adds a visual element. You can see someone using their hands while they talk and observe their facial expressions. Video adds depth to a discussion by incorporating multiple senses (such as sight and sound).

AVOIDING VIDEO FATIGUE

To avoid video fatigue and overload, use webcams only when they enhance the learning. Here are three ways to use webcams in a virtual class without adding to the challenge.

1. Turn the cameras on and off at set times during a virtual class. For example, start with them on during the introductions and opening activities, turn them off while brainstorming solutions to a problem, and then turn them on again for the debrief discussion. Getting comfortable with the video on/off switch keeps the tool fresh and interesting.

2. Teach participants how to use the video settings. Most platforms include a "hide self-view" option. Teach attendees how to use it so they aren't fixated on watching themselves on camera.

3. Transform thinking about perfection. Encourage participants to use the "blur" or virtual background feature if they want to mask their surroundings. Show them how to adjust for low lighting or use virtual filters. Normalize having less-than-perfect appearances, and instead focus on the personal connection they provide.

In addition, webcams allow another form of participant input. For example, participants can use their cameras to demonstrate proficiency of a task. Or they can use filters and virtual backgrounds to express themselves. For instance, in one of my recent virtual classes, the participants worked in teams throughout the program on a continuous case study. After the first breakout activity, one group returned to the main room with matching virtual backgrounds. They put together a team identity, adding an element of fun and sense of shared experience to the program. After seeing the first team do it, many of the other groups followed suit. It fostered a sense of shared account-ability and contributed to higher engagement levels in the program.

ENCOURAGING PARTICIPANT USE OF WEBCAMS

A common complaint among virtual facilitators is participants who don't turn on their webcams. To overcome this obstacle, use the following techniques:

- Mention any webcam requirements in the program description.
- Share webcam expectations in all preprogram communications.
- Remind participants to open their webcams at the start of each virtual class.
- Use the tips for avoiding video fatigue in this chapter.
- Teach participants how to use video tools, such as hide self-view and blur background.
- Invite (instead of require) webcam use.
- Recognize and accept that some participants may have valid reasons for keeping their cameras off.

Breakout Rooms

Breakout rooms used to be a feature limited to online "training" platforms, but they are now available in nearly every virtual classroom product. In case you're not familiar with breakouts, they let you facilitate small group activities in a virtual class similar to how they would work in the in-person session. Participants can divide into smaller groups and go into a smaller sub-conferencing space (the breakout room). Only those in the breakout can hear and see one another.

The modern breakout room has new features that give facilitators more granular control over the experience. Today's breakouts have built-in timers, video capabilities, broadcast messages, and countdown clocks. Depending on the platform, participants can either be assigned to a room or choose which breakout room to join. At least one platform, Adobe Connect, allows the host to quickly "rotate" groups from one breakout room to another, which is a fast way to move from one activity to the next. In addition, breakout rooms are easier to use now than they were in the past—in most platforms, it's just a click or two of a button to establish and create them. Overall, the breakout experience is now much more seamless for everyone.

The biggest benefit of breakout rooms is the community they can create. They encourage social connection in ways not as easily attainable in a larger group size and they provide space for participants to have more meaningful conversations. Individuals can use these rooms to pair up for discussions or work in small groups on relevant activities.

While it's tempting to stay anonymous in a large audience, it's much harder to hide in a small group when everyone is expected to participate. For example, it's common for my 90-minute virtual workshops to have at least four or five small-group discussions in breakouts (Figure 3-5). This collaboration contributes to a participant-centered immersive learning experience.

Virtual Reality and Augmented Reality Tools

Several vendors either already have or are on the edge of building virtual reality and/or augmented reality elements into their virtual classroom platforms. When the original Microsoft HoloLens device first integrated with Microsoft Skype for immersive online meetings, it set the course for others to follow. The ability to easily transfer from the virtual classroom into a virtual simulation is now becoming commonplace in many platforms. And, as mentioned earlier, several platforms now have hand-gesture recognition, which incorporates augmented features into a conversation.

Video filters and studio effects are other examples of using augmented reality in a virtual classroom. They add digital elements to a video stream, from frames to accessories to virtual makeup. In addition, collaborative whiteboards and other training tools are integrating with virtual reality meeting spaces. These features are rapidly evolving, and we will explore them in more detail in chapters 6 and 7.

FIGURE 3-5. Example of Breakouts in Zoom

A Final Word About Virtual Tools

Despite the heavy emphasis just placed on the updated tool set available in today's virtual classrooms, it's essential to remember that it's not *only* about the tools. It's not even about using them for participant engagement. Instead, the number one goal of the learning experience is always to learn and apply the new knowledge and skills back on the job. It's all about the learning and the learning transfer. Virtual classroom tools are a means to accomplish this goal. They can jump-start meaningful conversations, provide avenues of communication, and allow for better feedback from the facilitator. They can even help create a more immersive experience, which can lead to behavior change.

In other words, there should never be a time when you use a tool just to use a tool. Activities for the sake of activities are not useful. For example, participants shouldn't be asked to type in chat just to ensure they are paying attention. And we shouldn't post a poll asking "Are you still there?" (Yes, I've seen that done in a virtual class!) Instead, every part of the virtual class should be coordinated toward the goal of learning. Tools are a pathway toward engagement, which in turn leads to learning and application. Therefore, let's keep them in proper perspective.

WHEN TO TEACH THE PLATFORM TOOLS?

If you're concerned about technology issues stemming from participants who don't know how to use the platform features, then make sure they have the information needed. As technology advances, this only becomes more important. We want the learners to focus on the content, not their frustration over a tool. There are three ways facilitators can teach participants how to use the platform's tools:

- **As a prerequisite.** Hold an orientation program that invites participants to test out their connections and get comfortable with the platform tools. A similar option is to invite participants to watch a prerecorded overview video of the platform. Or send a how-to guide with screenshots, which they can refer to during log in and throughout the program.
- **At the start time.** Use the first few minutes of the class to walk through the tools and how to use them. Note that this type of opening could be

boring for anyone who is already familiar with the tools, and could lead to them tuning out and not tuning back in.

- **In the moment.** At the time each tool is used, spend a moment sharing how to find the tool and how to use it. Plan the activity so that those using the tool for the first time can get a little practice before proceeding to the activity. My preferred method is a combination of the first and last options. I want to equip participants in advance, and also remind them how to use the tools in the moment.

Relevant Skill Set:
Facilitating Immersive Virtual Classes

Once you have a current mindset and an updated tool set, it's time to apply the relevant skill set for immersive virtual classes. The goal is to create an *immersive participant experience full of meaningful and relevant engagement.* These conditions are enabled by the available tools and established by a dedicated, skilled, modern virtual facilitator who sets everyone up for success. One who creates a learning environment that allows participants to fully engage and skillfully involves participants in the program and leads them along the learning path.

However, from the facilitator's perspective, it can be especially difficult to facilitate well if your audience shows up and then shuts down. You may feel all alone, especially if you are isolated in a home office or other room by yourself. It takes effort, and skill, to always focus on the audience and their learning journey. Placing the priority on participant engagement and learning must begin from the start.

Think back to virtual classes you've participated in before. When is the last time you could say you were truly immersed and not distracted by your surroundings? If it's happened recently, then you are one of the few fortunate ones. When teaching my virtual facilitation skills workshop, I always ask participants to share "one word to describe your experience as a participant in most virtual classes." Figure 3-6 shows a sampling of the most common responses.

FIGURE 3-6. Words That Describe the Typical Participant Experience

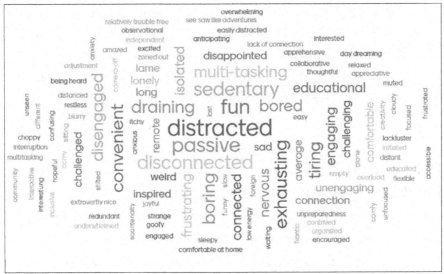

To create an interactive and engaging virtual class that's full of meaningful dialogue and discussion, we must ensure it's set up that way from the outset. Remember, you are interrupting someone in the middle of the workday, when they are surrounded by distractions, and asking them to join a virtual event and focus on learning. To do this well, the learner needs to experience a distinct transition between working and learning at the start of a virtual class. The way it begins determines the way it will go.

Assuming the stage is set for engagement and involvement, the facilitator can then proceed to create a successful learning environment. In fact, nine facilitator skills are needed for immersive and engaging virtual classes:

- ▶ Build rapport.
- ▶ Show up on video.
- ▶ Read the virtual room.
- ▶ Have a clear voice.
- ▶ Manage group dynamics.
- ▶ Release control to participants.

- ▶ Debrief activities.
- ▶ Multitask to the max.
- ▶ Validate learning.

These are the practical application steps for virtual classroom facilitators who adopt the learning experience facilitator mindset, which is in line with the skills introduced in chapter 2.

1. Build Rapport With and Among Participants

The best facilitators place their full emphasis on participants in the virtual classroom. They recognize the importance of connection and communication, shining the spotlight on participant input. They intentionally build rapport with learners, striving to make a good first impression and following up with authentic interest. As the saying goes, people don't care until they know how much you care. Showing a vested interest in each participant goes a long way toward them feeling like they're part of the group and engaged in the learning experience.

There are two common misconceptions about building rapport with an audience:

- ▶ I don't have time for it because there's too much content to cover.
- ▶ I don't do icebreakers because they are a waste of time.

Both sentiments have a hint of truth in them, but neither is true. And both can be overcome.

First, regarding time, if there's too much content to cover, then the program has a design problem. It's important to make space for conversation, so put relationship building on the agenda. The benefit of meeting synchronously is being together, so include time for social connections and discussion. If you're not planning to have interaction, then stick to an asynchronous program.

Second, if you don't like icebreakers, use openers instead. Openers serve a similar purpose—to break preoccupation with outside influences and capture attention in the virtual classroom. However, instead of posing a random get-to-know-you question, openers use content-related discussion starters. They tie directly to the program content.

For example, start a customer service virtual training class by asking, "What is your favorite restaurant and why?" to start building rapport, rather than, "What did you have for dinner last night?" Then use this question to generate discussion about the customer service experience in restaurants and move right into discussing the training-related topic. The opener serves as an advance organizer instead of a time-filler.

One of the best ways to build rapport with an audience is to ask questions—ask participants about themselves, their experience, their work, or their interest in the program. Use active listening skills to hear what they say, reflect upon their comments, and ask appropriate follow-on questions.

Another way to build rapport is to be relatable by finding things you have in common. If you've met before, refer back to the previous encounter. Or use current events to establish a shared connection.

THE ABCs OF BUILDING RAPPORT
- Ask questions.
- Be relatable.
- Create common connections.

Perhaps more important than building rapport between you and the participants is finding ways to create a shared online experience for the audience. This helps them realize that even though they are physically separated, they are together in an online room. Look for opportunities for participants to associate with one another. The online program already provides a connection; now let them explore what else they have in common.

No matter how powerful technology gets, there's nothing more immersive than the human connection that occurs during learning.

2. Show Up on Video
One of the fastest ways to build rapport between and among participants is to use the webcams. It's one of the best methods to increase communication

and dialogue in a group because of the visuals, body language, eye contact, and human connection that video can provide. And as mentioned earlier, using video allows for incorporating immersive augmented reality.

In my experience, the most engaging virtual classes have everyone on video at the start of the event. However, regardless of whether participants use webcams, the facilitator should be well versed in how to use video to enhance the learning experience. At minimum, the facilitator should be on camera to greet incoming participants. Your ability to "show up" on camera influences the group dynamic and sets the tone for collaboration.

To show up well, first consider your video setup. It doesn't matter if you sit or stand on camera, or a combination of both, just have the camera positioned at eye level. It's important not to appear as if you're looking down on everyone. If you're struggling to find the right angle, lighting, or distance, get creative with your equipment. For example, reposition your laptop to a different location, or use a mobile device perched on a tripod as your webcam connection to the virtual classroom.

FIGURE 3-7. Example of Proper Camera Angle

A common concern about being on camera is how to maintain eye contact while facilitating. First, remember that as a learning experience facilitator, you're likely not reading from a script or teleprompter. Instead, you're leading a discussion or having a conversation with participants. Therefore, look into the camera lens when other people are talking to demonstrate active listening skills. There will be natural times to glance away from the lens, just like glancing in a rearview mirror while driving a car. You can look at your facilitation notes or catch up on chat conversations while participants are working on an activity. Set up your delivery space in a way where you can easily see the entire screen at the same time as the camera lens.

CAMERA CONSIDERATIONS
- **Put the webcam at eye level.** Move your webcam to a spot that centers your face onscreen instead of looking down at it.
- **Place lighting in front.** Have a light source in front of you instead of to the side or behind you.
- **Position yourself the correct distance.** Sit far enough away from the camera that your shoulders are visible and your eyes are about a third of the way down the screen.

3. Read the Virtual Room

I frequently hear frustration from virtual facilitators who think that online classes are difficult because they lack "body language." Using the webcams can partially overcome this challenge. However, there's a better response: Shift your mindset to think about reading the room in other ways. The best virtual presenters can read a virtual room even if no one is on the webcam. They simply use other techniques to gather feedback on participant engagement and learning.

It may seem more difficult to do that in a virtual classroom, but it's really not. You still observe the environment by watching for cues and paying attention to detail. Carefully observe the audience and their actions. Look for inputs—either verbal or physical (typing in chat, writing on the white-board, responding to poll questions)—and actively listen to those responses. If participants are on camera, you can also watch their facial expressions and reactions.

If you are feeling uncertain about the cues, interpreting them the wrong way, or thinking you may be off because of cultural differences, simply ask the group for feedback. Post a poll question to gauge how participants are feeling about a topic. Encourage the use of emojis and chat. Invite them to verbally share their thoughts or express them on a white-board. Then use this input to adjust your facilitation style accordingly. For example, if energy levels have dropped, take a short stretch break to revitalize the room. It's okay to say something like, "This has been a productive conversation. Let's take a quick break from looking at the screen. I recommend you stand up and reach your arms overhead, turn your head from side to side, or shake out your fingers—do something to get your body moving!" By paying close attention to your participants, you can "read" their digital cues and adapt appropriately.

4. Have a Clear Voice

The facilitator's voice in a virtual class has a direct impact on the participants' ability to focus and learn. Your voice needs to be strong, easy to hear, and easy to understand. If you're familiar with FM radio transmitters, think back to a time when static prevented you from clearly hearing a song. Or when poor cell service led to a bad phone connection. It is disruptive and distracting. It's the same thing when a facilitator's voice is not clear. Even though your goal is to share airtime and get the participants talking, your own audio establishes the baseline. In fact, a recent study discovered that highly qualified subject matter experts were perceived as having poor credibility when their audio stream wasn't clear (McKinlay 2021). Same message, same content, same speaker—the only variable was audio quality. It pays to ensure your audio is as crystal clear as it can be.

There are two components to having good audio: the equipment used and the speaker's voice. These elements are important for both facilitators and participants, but we'll focus on the facilitator for now.

My number one equipment recommendation for any virtual facilitator is to use a wired headset or wired external microphone. The audio quality of an external microphone is almost always far superior to a device's built-in mic. Some facilitators have told me that they avoid using headsets because they don't want to have a heavy band over their head or thick speakers over their ears. However, if this is why you're avoiding them, you should investigate a different style, such as a behind-the-neck headset or a standing desktop microphone. When using a headset, position the microphone so it doesn't catch your breath while speaking; otherwise it'll sound like you're in an air tunnel. In addition, most modern virtual classroom platforms include built-in noise-canceling features. Get familiar with these controls and how to use them.

If you're using computer-based audio (VoIP) and you're having bandwidth challenges, switch to a telephone connection. Or take steps to reduce your bandwidth needs by shutting down other programs, prioritizing your device on the network, or turning off your webcam. Participants will be more forgiving of poor video than they will poor audio quality.

Regarding your voice, it should be crisp, easy to understand, and neutral without using filler words. It should also be energetic so that your enthusiasm comes through the computer screen. According to one research study, a positive tone will enhance the learning experience (Bliss-Moreau, Owren, and Barrett 2010).

Speaking of tone, if you've never heard a recording of your own voice, make a point to do so. Listen to see if you have vocal variety and emphasize the appropriate words. Remember that listening to a monotone or difficult-to-hear speaker is exhausting in an in-person environment, and it's even worse when online. Use a pleasant, melodic vocal tone for best results.

Perhaps more important than voice tone are the words you speak. A well-known scripture says, "Do not use harmful words, only helpful words" (Ephesians 4:29, GNT). Beyond any religious connotation, this is sage advice for virtual facilitators who are enabling others to learn. Consider how your sentences are phrased—are you using positive, encouraging words when talking with a participant? How often are you complimenting efforts, expressing confidence, and inspiring the group with affirmative feedback? Take every opportunity to praise participants, use positive words, and encourage them.

5. Manage Group Dynamics

An immersive learning environment—with full focus on the participants and their learning experience—will incorporate robust discussion and interaction among individuals. Therefore, facilitators need to be able to effectively manage group dynamics. This includes everything from motivating the group to continue learning, to keeping track of time and process, to managing the planned learning activities. At the same time, facilitators need to build trust, encourage dialogue, and build consensus with the group.

Participant motivation can come from internal or external sources. When internally motivated, participants will want to engage and learn because of their interest in the topic or the realization of how it benefits them. Externally motivated participants, on the other hand, may be driven by a job requirement, an organizational mandate, or some other outside influence. Facilitators can provide an immediate positive influence on participants' external motivation by clearly sharing the WIIFM ("What's in it for me?") of the content and helping participants understand the benefits. In addition, facilitators can share relevant examples and ways to immediately apply the learning content back on the job. The facilitator's actions and words can be a key external influence on participant motivation.

Effective facilitators also ensure that they are providing clear activity instructions and expectations. They never leave participants wondering what to do, when to do it, or what their current task entails. It's not that the facilitator becomes dictatorial in nature; it's that they are a clear communicator. If the activity's instructions are lengthy or detailed, they're best shared in smaller chunks, both visually and verbally.

In addition, facilitators need to keep track of time. Because virtual classes are usually 60 to 90 minutes long (or shorter), every minute counts. Even a five-minute unexpected delay can affect the program flow. During discussions, skilled facilitators should actively listen while monitoring input signals (such as time and topics). They may need to shorten a conversation, place a topic in the parking lot for later discussion, or ask permission to take the group in a different direction.

FACILITATOR SKILLS TO MANAGE GROUP DYNAMICS
- Establish group guidelines.
- Tap into participant motivation.
- Provide clear activity instructions.
- Keep track of time.
- Include everyone when phrasing questions.
- Assign partners and teams with intention.

Skilled facilitators also use techniques to ensure everyone is included in activities, such as by deliberately phrasing questions to invite all to participate. Instead of asking, "Who else has a comment about this topic?" and waiting for responses, they might say, "Raise your hand if you have a comment; otherwise click on the 'no' emoji." Or they could say, "There are 11 of you, so let's get 11 responses in chat before we continue." By keeping track of participation and openly asking for input, skilled facilitators seek everyone's involvement in the learning.

Good group dynamics are established at the beginning of a virtual class and supported by the facilitator. This includes setting guidelines at the start and gaining buy-in on expectations. For example, when we talk about participation guidelines at the start of my virtual classes, I'll sometimes ask participants to "manage the distractions they can, and minimize the ones they can't," and then invite them to choose an emoji to symbolize their agreement. Other times, I'll ask participants to choose their role for the class, with options such as "chat champion," "hand-raise monitor," "notetaker," and "active participant." Or, I might propose a set of participation standards and invite the group to comment on and adjust them before we put them to a vote. Regardless of the method used, the intent is to gain agreement on how the group will work together to achieve the learning goals.

Another technique to manage group dynamics is to assign partners or teams with intention. For example, it may make sense to group participants by region or department in one class, while another class is better served by diversifying the groups. Skilled facilitators pay attention to how well groups "gel" together and adjust accordingly. It's helpful to purposefully assign a team leader during breakout activities so the group doesn't waste time figuring out roles and responsibilities. For example, simply saying, "As we transition into breakout groups, if your name is alphabetically listed first in your breakout room's participant list, please jump in to be the team leader. That means you get to talk first and help the group keep track of time."

Typically, if a skilled facilitator successfully manages group dynamics in the virtual classroom, the participants won't notice it. It becomes part of the overall learning experience.

6. Release Control to Participants

One of the most important yet most difficult skills for a learning experience facilitator to master is the ability to release control to participants. Letting go of the need to be in power and allowing it to shift to participants can be challenging to do in person, and it's even tougher to do online. Adding in the virtual element, where participants may not be visible and it's harder to know if they are engaged, creates an extra hurdle for many facilitators.

A common reason behind the hesitancy to release control to remote participants is the facilitator's fear of silence. However, a well-designed, relevant class full of interaction and discussion will keep participants involved. Some facilitators also fear silence because they think they aren't doing their job if they aren't talking. As a result, a common mistake is to keep a running commentary going while participants are doing an activity; for example, when the facilitator starts talking about the first item to appear on the whiteboard during a brainstorming activity. Or when facilitators start reading comments when participants are responding to a question via chat. Remember, no one is listening because they are typing in their own responses and reading the others. Skilled facilitators are comfortable with silence while participants focus on their work.

Silence is also a good technique to help participants learn. Think of silence for the brain like sleep for our bodies. It's a necessity, and provides a chance to renew and recharge. The best virtual classes incorporate silence as a learning tool by providing reflection time.

Two key facilitation methods that involve releasing control to participants are to share airtime and allow choice:

- **Share airtime.** Effective facilitators actively look for ways to involve participants in the discussion. They rarely—if ever—read exactly what's written on a slide. They may post a slide and ask participants to raise their hand when finished reading it, or ask participants to comment on the content, but they don't just read it aloud to hear themselves talk.

- **Allow choice.** Facilitators recognize that most adults don't like to be told what to do, and instead prefer to have a say over their environment. Therefore, skilled facilitators give participants a choice at every possible opportunity. This can be as simple as using an invitation instead of a command (for example, "Please join me on page 7 to review the case study instructions."). Or it can be more complex, like letting participants choose which case study to use in their small group work. Another option is taking advantage of the modern virtual classroom's "choose your own breakout room" feature.

For my own virtual classes, I preplan ways to release control to the participants. I go through the facilitator guide looking for opportunities to open up the dialogue. I review the slides to see where there might be too much lecture. I search for ways to involve the learners and provide choices. And afterward, I reflect back on the experience to see where I could have improved. My goal is always to keep the participants immersed in the conversation and collaboration so they can learn from one another and apply the content.

7. Debrief Learning Activities

A classic facilitator responsibility is to guide participants through an experience, followed by helping them process and learn from it. Skilled facilitators ask a series of intentional questions designed to help participants reflect and respond. This process is called "debriefing," and it's an essential facilitator task. We'll even revisit it in almost every chapter of this book because it fits into every learning environment.

There are several ways to lead a debrief discussion. One common technique is to ask a series of questions: "What?" "So what?" and "Now what?" (Driscoll and Teh 2001). In this method, the facilitator asks participants to reflect on what actually happened during the learning experience. Then they ask questions about the importance of the experience, and finally to probe around the application opportunities. Another technique is to simply ask reflection questions, such as "What's a new insight you have gained?" and "How will you apply this information?"

The common thread for all debriefing techniques is asking questions to encourage contemplation, reflection, and learning. However, while a facilitator's primary role in debriefing activities isn't unique to the virtual classroom, the debriefing skill manifests slightly differently in various places.

For now, we will focus on how to debrief in the immersive virtual classroom. The uniqueness of the virtual classroom involves keeping participant attention during what could become a lengthy debrief discussion. If only one person is speaking at a time, everyone else may be tempted to tune out of the conversation. A skilled facilitator keeps people engaged during the debrief by asking for responses from the entire group (such as via chat or poll). They may also use guided breakout group conversations during which participants process the learning experience on their own in small teams. When facilitators pay extra attention to the timing and amount of time spent on debrief questions, they can create an appropriate balance of conversation time to keep energy and engagement levels high.

Another distinction in the virtual classroom is the number of tools available. The ease of involving everyone in polling, chatting, whiteboarding, and breakouts creates the opportunity to include everyone in the debrief discussions. It also allows for creative debrief methods. For example, after a whiteboard brainstorm, debrief by asking participants to review the board and mark or stamp anything that resonates with them. That way, participants can silently review the class input and reflect upon it. Once the stamps appear, ask the group to look for patterns and themes, drawing out key learning points from their observations.

Speaking of whiteboards, they are one of my favorite tools to use when debriefing, because you can post questions in various sections of the board and invite responses. Participants can review the questions and respond individually.

When participants return from breakout activities, several techniques work well for the debrief. The round robin "report out" method is most common: "Let's hear first from Group 1, then from Group 2, then Group 3, and so on." However, I recommend avoiding that method if you want to keep engagement levels high.

Instead, I use one of these methods to debrief breakouts:
- Invite each group to share one highlight from their discussion, avoiding anything that has already been said by another group. Instruct all participants to "raise hand" if they hear something that their group also discussed.

- Post a poll question with common discussion topics that likely surfaced during the breakout activity. Invite participants to select which topics their group discussed, and then reveal the post-poll results and patterns. Be sure to include "other" as a response option to capture the remaining unique topics.
- Invite each group to share their whiteboard or other electronic notes, asking their spokesperson to "highlight one place on your board we should look."
- In a shared collaborative whiteboard, conduct a digital "gallery walk," where each group can scroll around the board reviewing what everyone else said. Then invite discussion of patterns and themes.

Traditionally, debrief questions are open ended in nature. However, in the virtual classroom environment, most open-ended questions are met with silence and usually aren't specific enough to jump-start a conversation. Virtual facilitators get much better responses when the initial question is both *precise* and *prescriptive*. In other words, it's a specific question that includes directions on how to respond. For example, instead of asking, "What did you observe in this demonstration?" it's better to say, "What one item did you observe in the demonstration? Please type it in chat." Or to say, "Raise your hand if you noticed ABC happen during the demonstration." From there, a facilitator can use the typed comments or raised hands to ask follow-on questions that get the conversation going.

Skilled facilitators who successfully debrief learning experiences in the virtual classroom are active listeners who can draw out meaning from both written and verbal comments. This allows them to keep participants immersed in the learning.

8. Multitask to the Max

Expert facilitators can seamlessly manage the technology while also facilitating the learning experience. Even if they have a co-facilitator, an assistant, or a producer, skilled facilitators can still multitask with ease. However, while multitasking may come naturally to a few tech-savvy facilitators, more often than not, it's a learned behavior.

Some of this ability comes from diligent practice—the more you do it, the easier it becomes. But most of this skill comes from a recognition that multitasking is just efficiently switching between multiple tasks. The faster you can switch between these things, the more seamless it appears. Kind of like typing on a keyboard. Some do it fast, others do it slow, but everyone presses just one key at a time.

Another way to think of it is like driving a car. You need to keep your eyes on the road in front of you, while also steering and navigating and avoiding collisions. To do this you also need to watch the dashboard, glance in the mirrors, and keep the car moving toward your destination. These tasks can seem overwhelming at first, but they become easier with time. It's the same in the virtual classroom. There is a lot going on, and many things to manage at once. However, whether from practice or from incorporating techniques that work for you, it eventually becomes seamless.

For example, I know my own limitation of typing while talking. No matter how much I practice, I simply cannot do it with ease. I need to pause and be silent while I type. So, I've learned to overcome this limitation by incorporating a few simple techniques. I have common phrases set up in my computer's "autocomplete" feature, so it fills in the rest when I type a shortcut key. I also keep an electronic notepad open on my laptop, which has pre-typed text that I know I'll need to use in chat during class. That way I can quickly copy and paste it into chat when needed. Finally, I know that if I have to post in chat during a virtual class, I go ahead and type while participants are occupied, simply waiting to press send until it's time. The point here is that I have created a strategy to help me be a better multitasker.

In addition, facilitators have an easier time multitasking when they're prepared. Technology problems can and will occur in the virtual classroom, leading to disruption. When these tech issues get in the way of learning, the facilitator can quickly switch to a backup plan to keep the class moving along. But only if they've prepared one. For example, if a poll unexpectedly fails to work, a facilitator who's aware and adept at multitasking can quickly react by launching another method to gather the input. They may say, "Out of these four options, which would you choose? Write down your response on paper and hold it up to the webcam so we can all see." Or if the whiteboard tools aren't working for all participants, a facilitator who's comfortable with multitasking might say, "For those of you who are struggling with the drawing tools, just type your responses in chat and I'll transfer them to the whiteboard for you." The more comfortable a facilitator is with task-switching, the less technology will get in the way of learning.

Another reason multitasking is important is that it allows facilitators to maintain an appropriate yet quick pace in the classroom. Multitasking facilitators keep participants actively immersed in activities that lead toward the learning outcomes. They keep the conversation moving along, looking for regular input and inviting frequent interaction. To do these things well, they must be adept at seamlessly switching between tasks.

THE PRODUCER ROLE

The best virtual classes include two session leaders: a skilled facilitator and an expert producer. The facilitator leads the learning experience, while the producer manages the technology. Some organizations refer to this role as the "host" or "moderator," especially if they have a speaking role. Producers support the facilitator by ensuring all activities run as planned, keeping track of time, and assisting in the background. Producers also support participants by creating a seamless technical experience for everyone involved. They help create and maintain the immersive environment by helping participants focus on the learning instead of the technology.

9. Validate Learning

The ultimate measure of a successful learning experience is the transfer of that learning to on-the-job results. This occurs when participants change their behavior by applying their newly learned skills. All of the virtual class activities and facilitation techniques should lead to these outcomes. Therefore, facilitators need to ensure that participants are following along the expected learning path. And they must recognize if participants are (or aren't) understanding and grasping the training topics so they can apply what they learn. Facilitators should also validate the participants' learning and their ability to apply it.

Therefore it is important for facilitators to build in knowledge checks throughout the event to assess understanding and comprehension. These should go beyond simple recall-type poll questions and quizzes and instead use relevant application questions or hands-on activities and other exercises. For example, in the "asking questions" section of my virtual facilitation skills workshops, each participant has to rephrase commonly asked questions according to the learned skill. This activity mirrors what they'll do when facilitating and helps me test their comprehension and application abilities.

Next, facilitators can use very small group breakout activities (two to three attendees per group) for application conversations. When working in pairs or trios, everyone has an opportunity to be involved and engaged. It's also much harder to stay silent when others rely on you.

Skilled virtual facilitators create extra examples and scenarios, in case participants have questions or need additional explanation. This ability to flex the agenda as needed if the audience needs more time on a topic comes from a combination of active listening and reading the room. Facilitators who have determined the "need to know" versus the "nice to know" content can more easily adjust a program's timing by spending less time on the less important information and more time where it counts.

Finally, facilitators should carefully monitor participant involvement in the learning activities. If there are 15 people in a virtual class, it isn't enough for only five of them to learn. All 15 are important. Because it is easier to hide and remain anonymous in a virtual class, facilitators need to ensure each person is connected and engaged so that they can learn. If participants choose to remain passive, find out if that choice is affecting their ability to learn. If technical problems get in the way of learning—such as a participant who can't stay connected to the class due to bandwidth issues—be ready to reschedule them to the next class or have back-up learning activities ready to send.

Albert Einstein purportedly once said, "I never teach my pupils; I only attempt to provide the conditions in which they learn." This famous quote summarizes the role of a skilled virtual facilitator—it is the unique combination of their mindset, tool set, and skill set that enables the conditions in which participants can thrive.

VOICES FROM THE FIELD

I have long valued the advice of Jay Cross, who championed the use of informal learning, where the majority of learning takes place. What is informal learning? It's those "holes" in your learning curriculum where people talk to one another and share what's worked for them and their challenges and concerns. In classroom training informal learning takes place before and after class, during breaks, and in small group activities. For remote learners, it's vital to capture that same thing, whether through small group discussions, case studies, application exercises, or simply paired chats. Facilitating ways for participants to connect allows for informal learning to happen, and that's key to providing a valuable learning experience. Don't miss the opportunity to plan informal learning in your programs.
—**Howard H. Prager, leadership coach, consultant, and author of** *Make Someone's Day: Becoming a Memorable Leader in Work and Life*

**FOUR MUST-DO STEPS TO CREATE
AN ENGAGING ENVIRONMENT**

Give these four steps a try in your next virtual class and you will see an immediate difference in audience engagement levels.

- **Set expectations.** Let everyone know in advance that the session will be an interactive experience, not a recorded presentation.
- **Start a conversation.** Greet everyone upon arrival and have an onscreen invitation to join in the conversation.
- **Create a social environment.** Quickly establish relationships and connections so participants benefit from being in a virtual room with others.
- **Seek frequent engagement.** Use the platform's tools to establish and maintain a brisk pace with ongoing involvement.

In Summary

This entire chapter can be summarized into three sentiments: collaboration, consideration, and conversation. When a facilitator changes their mindset to fully focus on participants and guide them through an experience, learning is more likely to occur. When the facilitator carefully considers their actions, and also rightfully considers the participant's perspective, learning is more likely to be the result. And when the facilitator invites and encourages conversation using both modern virtual classroom tools and their communication skills, learning will be at the forefront of the learning experience.

Self-Assessment:
Facilitating Immersive Virtual Classes

Skill	Your Self-Assessment				
	Needs Improvement		Partially Proficient		Already Mastered
Build rapport	☐	☐	☐	☐	☐
Show up on video	☐	☐	☐	☐	☐
Read the virtual room	☐	☐	☐	☐	☐
Have a clear and authentic voice	☐	☐	☐	☐	☐
Manage group dynamics	☐	☐	☐	☐	☐
Release control to participants	☐	☐	☐	☐	☐
Debrief activities	☐	☐	☐	☐	☐
Multitask to the max	☐	☐	☐	☐	☐
Validate learning	☐	☐	☐	☐	☐

For the skills noted as anything less than "already mastered," set goals for improvement, one step at a time.

CHAPTER 4
Facilitating Hybrid Classes

In the wake of the COVID-19 pandemic, organizations turned to hybrid working models as a way to accommodate both in-office and remote employees. A McKinsey study revealed that nine out of 10 organizations planned to adopt a hybrid working model, and most executives did not expect their employees to be in the office every day of the week (Alexander et al. 2021).

As a result, organizations have been faced with decisions about how to handle in-person training classes. For some, it is a simple decision to go back to the classroom. For others, it is easy to continue virtual learning. But many organizations find themselves needing to create a third option: allowing some participants to be in person, with the rest online. This is called a hybrid class—when participants are not all in the same location. The mixed audiences are then connected by the virtual classroom platform.

In my 2021 survey, I asked, "What is your plan for facilitating hybrid training classes?" Of the 700 global training professionals who responded, 62 percent said they either were already facilitating them or would be facilitating them in the future (Huggett 2021). That's a significant number that I expect will only increase in future years as hybrid-working models become the norm.

In the past, I would have advised you to avoid this situation. In the section on designing and delivering hybrid classes in my 2016 virtual training book, I simply wrote "don't do it," before expanding upon how to do it well. It's because the participant experience is vastly different in a hybrid environment—some are together in the classroom while others are isolated. However, because the hybrid classroom is a necessity for many organizations, learning experience facilitators should be equipped and prepared. It takes a specialized facilitation approach to simultaneously meet participant needs in those two unique environments.

Challenges of Hybrid Learning

The main challenge of the hybrid classroom is the different experience that virtual and in-person attendees have. The in-person audience benefits from being together and with the facilitator. The remote participants benefit from the robust software tools provided by the virtual classroom software; however, they're also isolated both from the group and from one another. Each experience has pros and cons. One isn't better than the other, but we need to pay attention to the differences if we want the learning experience to be successful.

For example, one of my favorite parts of facilitating is getting to know the participants better. To hear their stories, discover their path, and uncover their reasons for participating in this particular learning experience. I also enjoy connecting participants with one another, encouraging networking and fostering relationships. For an in-person class, these conversations begin as participants enter the room and continue throughout the program. For virtual classes, these discussions are deliberate as I intentionally build in time for small talk. But in many hybrid classes, these beneficial conversations don't happen. The in-person participants can easily turn to the person next to them, while the remote attendees have to rely on the virtual classroom's single audio channel. It can be challenging to bridge the gap.

Another common activity in many learning experiences is small group collaboration. When in person, the participants can split into teams and use chart paper to brainstorm together. In a virtual class, breakout rooms with whiteboards serve the same purpose. But in a hybrid class, questions arise about how to organize the small groups, and what drawing tools are available to all. It takes significant prior planning and administrative effort to make this type of essential activity work.

These are just a few examples of the many challenges we encounter in creating effective hybrid classes. So now that they're here to stay, how do we make them successful?

Making Hybrid Learning Work

Skilled facilitators can make any learning program in any environment a positive experience for participants. Give them the bare-necessity tools and they will create an excellent experience that gets results. I once planned a very interactive course full of small group exercises, only to discover that my assigned location was a small boardroom filled mostly by a large, immovable table—there was barely room to walk around let alone facilitate the activities. Yet through creative modification and lots of adaptation, I made it work. The participants walked away with new knowledge and skills that they could apply immediately.

Of course, the best learning experiences are made up of more than "make it work" moments. For hybrid learning to be successful, it takes thoughtful planning and engaging facilitation. It also takes participants who are enabled and encouraged to actively immerse themselves in the learning experience regardless of their location.

Just like hybrid working is a new path for organizations, hybrid learning is a new model of workplace learning. Through intentional design and skilled facilitation, it can be done well. The rest of this chapter will explain how.

A WORKAROUND FOR HYBRID LEARNING

If you want to avoid hybrid learning and have the resources to continue supporting separate in-person and virtual classroom experiences, here's a straightforward solution: Design two separate but parallel learning experiences.

I did this for a global client who was willing to invest significant amounts of time and resources into their manager development training program. We created one fully classroom-based learning journey; the other was fully virtual. Both programs had the same learning objectives and generally the same activities. Participants were able to choose which experience they wanted. We met the needs of both audiences and avoided hybrid learning. This solution might not be the right one for your organization, but it's worth considering if you can.

Preparing to Facilitate Hybrid Learning

Facilitators play such a large role in creating a successful hybrid learning experience for participants. Even though the participants are "in charge" of their own learning, it's the facilitator who creates the environment where that learning happens. This fact couldn't be more true than in hybrid learning.

It starts with the facilitator's advance preparation. For an in-person class, facilitator preparation largely focuses on content. They need to learn the material, plan the activities, and tailor everything for the audience. For a virtual class, the focus shifts to technology. All the traditional preparation steps are still important, but platform planning takes center stage. Facilitators need to set the virtual classroom tools and activities in advance and communicate participant technology needs.

But the hybrid environment requires a different type of preparation. Now the emphasis needs to be on the participant experience—on creating an atmosphere that equalizes the participant experience despite their physical location. The facilitator needs to ensure that everyone has what they need in advance of the hybrid class, and that all expectations have been established (Figure 4-1).

A hybrid facilitator's advance preparation should include at least the following:

- ▶ Preparing the in-person hybrid classroom, to ensure it has a setup conducive for mixed-audience collaboration.
- ▶ Preparing the virtual classroom that will be used to connect the mixed audiences via audio, video, and other interactive features.

- Preparing the participants so that all are clear on expectations and also to ensure that remote attendees are ready with webcams and that in-person attendees bring their devices.

All three of these items should be viewed through the lens of the participant experience. The goal is to equalize the environment as much as possible so that learning can occur.

FIGURE 4-1. Comparison of Preparation Emphasis in Learning Modalities

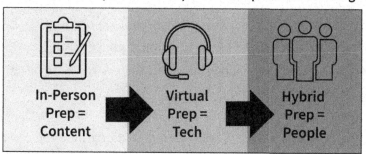

I often compare facilitator preparation to an Olympic athlete getting ready to compete in the games. These athletes are some of the most prepared people on the planet and most have spent years honing their craft. They frequently practice, learn from their mistakes, and leave nothing to chance. They bring extra equipment, like an additional pair of shoes or a second swimsuit, just in case. Their goal is to be the best they can be, under any circumstance.

Hybrid facilitators do not need to prepare quite as much as an elite athlete; however, there are lessons to be learned from their methods. At the end of this chapter, you'll find an updated version of my popular "Extra-Prepared

FACILITATION TIP

Invite each participant, regardless of location, to individually join the virtual classroom. This allows everyone to type in chat, respond to polls, and use the electronic input tools. Using a common platform will help equalize the learning experience.

Virtual Trainer Checklist," which first appeared in my 2010 book, *Virtual Training Basics*. It's a comprehensive list—Olympic athlete style—for hybrid facilitator preparation.

Helping Hands in Hybrid Learning

Rarely is a hybrid class led by just one person. The best hybrid learning experiences are supported and enriched by a full cast of characters. The roles may be determined in advance as part of the preparation or they may be selected by participants at the start of the program. I prefer getting participants involved in most responsibilities because it increases their engagement and contributes to their learning.

It's easy to assume that the facilitator is physically present in the classroom during a hybrid learning event. However, that's not always the case. The facilitator may be the only one who is off-site, with all participants in the classroom. Or it may be a mix of in-person and remote participants, with the facilitator also joining remotely. Another configuration could be multiple participants in one location, another group of participants in a second location, and still more participants joining individually via virtual classroom. To qualify as hybrid learning, it just means that not everyone is in the same location. This variety makes it all the more important to foster a team effort to create an ideal learning experience for all.

Let's start by reviewing some typical roles that make up this hybrid classroom team, and then we'll go a bit deeper into a few:

- ▶ **Learning experience facilitator.** Guides participants along a journey of self-directed discovery, leading to learning results and tangible outcomes. They help create and shape a positive learning environment.
- ▶ **Producer or tech troubleshooter.** Responsible for behind-the-scenes technical support and partnering with the facilitators and participants to help with any technology needs.

- **In-room moderator.** Responsible for the in-room activities during hybrid classes, and for helping engage all attendees. Assists with in-room facilitation if the facilitator is remote.
- **Scribe.** Responsible for typing in chat (or another electronic note-keeping tool) during appropriate times in the learning experience. This role may be automated by a virtual platform's AI-driven technology.
- **Chat and/or hand-raise monitor.** Responsible for keeping an eye on platform input tools (such as chat and raise hand) so that remote participants can be quickly acknowledged. This role may fall to the producer, or it could be a designated in-room participant.
- **Remote partner.** An in-room participant who serves as a "buddy" to remote participants, helping them see and hear everything going on in the room.

Experienced virtual facilitators recognize the importance of the producer's role in the hybrid class. The producer, for example, may be a co-facilitator who is involved with the program delivery. While one co-facilitator takes their turn leading the discussion and collaboration, the other is producing, and vice versa. Or, the producer may be a designated technology specialist who is responsible for making the tech run smoothly. Their priorities are helping remote participants get (and stay) connected to the classroom and ensuring in-person attendees have access to the online tools. They're also responsible for opening poll questions, opening online whiteboards, enabling breakout rooms, and assisting with other tools as needed. When tech challenges arise during the program, the producer troubleshoots and works to solve the problem.

The essential role of the producer is even more pronounced in hybrid learning. While it's possible for one facilitator to take on all the responsibility, their ability to be fully present in the learning experience will be hampered. It's difficult for one person to facilitate, support, engage, and troubleshoot all at the same time.

In addition to a producer, it's also helpful to designate an in-room moderator in each classroom location with a group of attendees. The in-room moderator's role is to assist with activities during the learning experience. They may pass out supplies, help keep track of time, or simply be the "eyes and ears" of the facilitator in the room. For example, if the facilitator needs to ask someone to move a webcam to a different location, write something on the physical whiteboard, or press "play" on a music device, they'll call upon the moderator for help.

In the most common hybrid learning setting, the facilitator is in the room with some participants, and the rest are joining remotely. In this situation, the facilitator or producer may act as the in-room moderator. However, if multiple groups of participants are together in various locations, an in-room moderator should be placed in each room. And if the facilitator is the only one who is remote, an in-room moderator is a must.

COMMON HYBRID CLASSROOM SCENARIOS
Any of the following configurations could be considered a hybrid class. In any of these scenarios, the main facilitator may be in person or remote:
- Most participants are co-located with some remote attendees.
- Most participants are remote with a few co-located attendees.
- Two (or more) co-located in-person groups.

One way to bridge the gap between different audiences in the hybrid classroom is to assign an in-room partner to each remote attendee. They can establish a private communication channel either by private chat in the virtual classroom or through some other method. The partnership benefits both, especially the remote attendees who may need extra assistance to feel included.

A few of the roles listed in this section help the facilitator release control of the learning to participants. As established in chapter 1, a learning experience facilitator serves as a guide instead of a presenter. Assigning roles to participants helps them take responsibility for their experience. It's a great way to get everyone involved. As one of my former managers told me, it's good for the participants to be as tired as you are at the end of the program—that means they were fully engaged.

Applying What You Already Know About Facilitation

Successful hybrid facilitation requires a combination of classroom facilitation skills and virtual facilitation skills. Facilitators who have done either of those things will recognize many of the requirements to be successful in a hybrid environment. They can take what they know about the former and apply it to the latter, then add in the distinctive features of hybrid environments.

These seven focus areas are specific to facilitators of hybrid learning:

- **Revise.** Review your content in advance to revise activities as needed to accommodate the mixed audience. For example, will some groups write on chart paper while others type in chat? And will some groups respond to questions by raising their actual hands while others use the "raise hand" button? How will you assign groups for a planned role-play activity?
- **Equalize.** Set up the learning experience to create equal access to learning activities for all participants. For example, have everyone join the virtual classroom using a device so that they can all respond to poll questions. Or ask everyone to be on camera for certain activities, including those who are in person.
- **Prioritize.** Place your emphasis and priority on the remote participants. For example, allow remote participants to talk first in a discussion. It's so easy to give the floor to the in-person audience in a conversation, so the deliberate attempt to draw in the off-site learners will create a sense of balance.

- **Normalize.** Focus on the common learning outcomes instead of the participant location differences. Whether they are online or in front of you, it's important to include and invite each person into the learning space. Normalize the experience for all regardless of their location. Make eye contact with all, invite everyone into the conversation, and focus on the overall learning experience.

- **Personalize.** Facilitators should also focus on each participant's involvement levels and attempt to draw everyone into the group discussions. Keep track of who is engaging, what questions they are asking, and what types of input they are giving. Assess their involvement, interest, and learning. Then adapt your facilitation methods accordingly to create a personalized approach. Offer extra insights, examples, feedback, and encouragement as needed.

- **Organize.** Finally, it's important to recognize the special technology requirements of the hybrid virtual classroom. Not only do you want everyone to be logged in to the virtual platform; you also want to ensure smooth connections and a seamless experience. Therefore, create organized technology guidelines for using tools, especially audio and video. For example, use only one audio connection for the in-person group to avoid echoes. Establish protocols for turning on webcams so that everyone can see. Have a producer or co-facilitator available to manage technology needs. By establishing these types of working guidelines, your program will be much more organized.

- **Supervise.** Its easy for participant conversations to spiral out of control in a hybrid class. Side conversations between in-person participants cause remote attendees to feel excluded. Remote participants may talk over one another when coming off mute, causing embarrassment or wasted time. For effective dialogue to occur, it takes established discussion guidelines with a facilitator who's able to supervise. We'll take a more detailed look at the "how-to" of this technique later in the chapter.

HYBRID CLASSROOM TECHNOLOGY

To accompany the global explosion of hybrid work, virtual platforms are rapidly developing tools to accommodate hybrid meeting and training environments. For example, some platforms now offer "companion mode" when joining a virtual event, to indicate they are co-located and don't need a separate audio connection. Many platforms are also offering new webcam viewing options to display remote participants in a more natural setting instead of boxes in rows and columns.

In addition to these software updates, many vendors have now introduced conference room hardware, such as intelligent swiveling cameras and enhanced microphones for better in-room audio. If your organization plans to adopt hybrid classrooms as part of your learning strategy, research the latest available tools for what you need. Invest in creating an ideal classroom setup to have the best possible mixed-audience hybrid learning experience.

Creating Clear Audio

We've talked about the importance of clear audio in other chapters, but in hybrid learning it simply must have top priority. Without quality audio, participants will not be able to hear one another and conversation will be stifled. The learning experience will suffer as a result.

Effective communication happens only when the audio connections are clear and easy to hear. Hybrid meeting facilitators should ensure that everyone in the physical room can be heard when speaking, and that remote attendees have clear audio connections.

To create clear audio, do the following five things:

▸ **Ensure every voice can be heard clearly.** Position microphones in the meeting room so that all can be heard. If needed, use multiple input sources, or ask participants to get closer to the mic when speaking.

▸ **Elevate sound by using wired connections.** Use wires for the best possible sound quality without interference. Wireless is great for distance and movement, but it's not always the best option for hybrid learners. Use wired microphones in the physical classroom and ask remote attendees to use wired headsets when possible for the highest quality sound.

▶ **Eliminate background noises.** Use the platform's noise-canceling features to eliminate extraneous noise. Have remote participants using headsets position their microphones so they don't pick up heavy breathing sounds or other distractions.

▶ **Educate remote participants on the bandwidth effect.** Assist remote attendees with strategies to reduce bandwidth consumption so that their sound is strong and clear. Of course, ensure all other internet-enabled apps and processes on their laptops are closed. Another option is to have them switch to a telephone connection, if possible.

▶ **Exude enthusiasm and energy.** Pour energy and enthusiasm into your voice so that you are easy to hear. Stay close to the microphone so your voice carries both in the classroom and across the internet. And remember to stay positive—a facilitator's positive tone helps create a better learning environment (Clark and Mayer 2016).

VOICES FROM THE FIELD

"Be able to see and hear everyone, whether they are in person or virtual, and make sure they can see and hear you." —**Sharon Wingron, CEO, DevelopPEOPLE**

Using Video in Hybrid Classes

Effective hybrid classes allow participants to see one another via video. Many of the same principles discussed in chapter 3 also apply in this context. However, the hybrid classroom does bring some additional video-related challenges. For example, because they are partially in person, hybrid classes tend to be longer than virtual classes. So how do you avoid video fatigue of remote participants? And as an in-room facilitator, how do you look at the camera lens without ignoring your in-person participants?

First, carefully determine when video will be required and when it will be optional, and then communicate these norms in advance. I think it's especially important to turn the cameras on at the start of any interactive learning experience to establish rapport and set the tone for conversation and collaboration. Follow the recommended guidelines from the previous chapter on avoiding video fatigue and using video with intention. Those principles still apply in hybrid classes. It's admittedly a delicate balance between the benefits of visual contact and the challenges of staring at a camera lens for hours on end.

An innovative feature found in several hybrid and virtual classroom platforms is an "immersive" video viewing mode. The idea behind this feature is to make video conversation feel more natural. So, instead of showing each video feed as a square on a digital dashboard, remote participants are displayed in unique configurations (Figure 4-2). These augmented displays can enhance the conversations and feel more immersive without contributing to cognitive overload.

FIGURE 4-2. Example Immersive Video Scene in Zoom

©Zoom Video Communications, Inc. Reprinted with permission.

When possible, arrange the in-person hybrid classroom rooms so that everyone is visible on the room's primary webcam. If you don't have a dedicated hybrid meeting space, this may take some creative rearranging. For example, you could use an additional portable external camera (like a mobile device on a tripod). As hybrid working establishes itself as a long-term strategy instead of a temporary fix for remote employees, classroom equipment conducive for hybrid audiences will become more commonplace. Until that time, do your best to set up the classroom for the best possible video viewing.

Figure 4-3 shows an example of a hybrid classroom setup designed by Barco, using its innovative weConnect software to create an equitable learning experience for all participants. You can see a full 360-degree view of a hybrid classroom using the QR code at the end of this chapter (Figure 4-4).

FIGURE 4-3. One of Barco's Hybrid Classrooms

Reprinted with permission of Barco.

As a general guideline, I recommend that facilitators look into the camera lens while speaking to keep their primary focus on remote attendees.

Although it may feel unnatural to look at a camera lens when there are participants right in front of you, it will look normal to the off-site participants who are watching on their screen. Of course, you'll also need to shift your gaze to the room and then back to the camera lens. It's like driving a car—sometimes you keep your attention on the road while occasionally glancing in your rearview mirror (like when you're on the interstate), sometimes you focus on the mirrors (like when you're backing up), and other times your eyes stay glued to the road (like when you're in traffic). The trick is to seamlessly switch between them. It takes practice and intentional effort.

Also, remember, if you're keeping the mindset of a learning experience facilitator, the participants will be doing most of the talking. Facilitators presenting on camera for long periods of time should be a rare circumstance in hybrid learning.

Leading Hybrid Discussions

One of a facilitator's classic responsibilities is to lead discussions among participants. In a hybrid learning experience, this means bringing a remote-first mindset into the dynamic. It also means providing more structure and direction to help the discussion thrive.

Left unchecked, a group discussion in a hybrid event could be dominated by in-room participants. With hybrid, there's always the possibility of audio lags, which can lead to participants talking over one another. It's easy for people to become frustrated if they don't feel like they're contributing to the conversation, and this can have detrimental effects on the learning outcomes.

Therefore, facilitators in a hybrid class need to be much more directive in their discussion tactics, by creating boundaries and guidelines. It's a combination of providing structure while still releasing control. Think of it like a raging fire burning inside a fireplace: The sturdy structure of the fireplace provides a safe place for the fire to burn. A hybrid facilitator's discussion tactics can create that same sense of safety for participants, allowing them to enjoy robust collaboration and conversation within the parameters of a structured environment.

Leading discussions in a hybrid class requires slightly different techniques from leading in-person or even virtual classes. Here are three specific facilitation strategies to use:

- ▸ **Establish the environment.** Near the start of the learning experience, propose ground rules or guidelines for conversation. These can be co-created by the group instead of presented to them. The goal is to be up front about expectations for communication and to gain agreement on them from all participants.

- ▸ **Ask specific questions.** Be precise when using discussion-starter prompts. Ask specific questions to start a conversation and include a precisely stated method for all to respond. Then pause to allow time for input. For example, ask, "Who has experienced this situation in the past? Click on the 'raise hand' button if you have or click on 'no' if you have not." After a pause for participants to respond, invite them to elaborate, starting with an off-site attendee.

- ▸ **Manage discussion.** It's tempting to just let participants free-form their conversation, and in many cases that's the appropriate facilitation approach. However, the conversation in a hybrid class will flourish when skilled facilitators manage it well. Simple techniques like establishing an order for responses will go a long way. Saying something like "First let's hear from Julia, then Liam, then from those here in the room" will help. Of course, remember the "remote first" mindset when seeking responses.

Manage Activities

The best learning experiences include the ability to work collaboratively in small groups. Breakout activities are a natural way to make this happen. In a traditional classroom, small groups of five to seven participants could partner up for an exercise. In a virtual classroom, small groups of three to four participants can work together in breakout rooms. But what about the hybrid learning environment? What's the best way to capitalize on collaboration while focusing on an inclusive learning experience?

Breakouts are still a helpful feature in a hybrid class, and I recommend using them. The biggest question is whether to put all remote participants together in a virtual breakout room and have the in-person participants separate into groups. This may be the easiest solution, but it's not always the best way to create an equal experience.

If you can plan breakout activities in advance, one option would be to reserve subconference rooms near the main classroom (assuming the building has them, of course!). Then at the time of the activity, assign a mixture of in-person and remote attendees to each group and send them all to the smaller breakout rooms. This strategy requires more advance planning and coordination but gives the best learning experience for all.

In one of my recent hybrid classes, only one participant joined remotely, and the rest were co-located in the room. So, we assigned her a seat in the room and ensured that she could see everyone in the room via video stream. For small group work, her assigned group took the room's laptop with them and set her in a seat (with all group members visible). She was able to participate just like everyone else. At the end of the day, she said that she felt included and part of the team throughout the experience.

VOICES FROM THE FIELD

"One of the biggest challenges of facilitating a hybrid class is the use of multiple technologies (both hardware and software). Try to keep the tech as simple as possible; the more bells and whistles you use, the more likely it is that something will fail. If you are not comfortable using multiple devices and/or software programs at the same time you are facilitating, only use the tech you are most confident using." —Maureen Orey, Founder and CEO, Workplace Learning and Performance Group

What's Next

Hybrid learning is new for many organizations, participants, and facilitators. It will take time and practice for everyone to become comfortable with this environment. Experiment in your organization with the best classroom setups, technology tools, and methods for collaboration. Keep an eye on new platform features that become available to help with hybrid learning. Test new hardware devices designed to help equalize

FIGURE 4-4. See Inside a Baraco Hybrid Classroom

the learning experience for all attendees. As organizations improve their hybrid working models, facilitators will need to rise to the occasion and provide effective hybrid learning environments. We are equipped to do it, and to do it well.

Checklist: The Extra-Prepared Hybrid Facilitator

Hybrid Event Details

☐ I have scheduled an in-person classroom for co-located participants.

☐ I have scheduled the classroom reservation to start at least 30 minutes prior to the class start time, to allot for tech testing and setup.

☐ I have scheduled the classroom reservation to start at least 60 minutes prior to the class start time, to allot for tech testing and extra setup.

☐ I have scheduled a virtual classroom connection to bridge the gap between on-site and off-site attendees.

☐ I have all connection links for the virtual classroom, including host, presenter, and participant links (if they are different).

☐ I have all event passcodes, including host, presenter, and participant codes (if they are different).

☐ If using a telephone conference device (such as an in-room audio system), I have all teleconference details, including moderator and participant codes.

Subtotal: _____

Hybrid Classroom Device Setup

☐ I have a reliable computer or laptop that I can use when facilitating hybrid classes.

☐ I have a second reliable computer, laptop, or mobile device that I can use as a "sidekick" (backup) when facilitating hybrid classes.

☐ All software, drivers, and plug-ins necessary to connect to the virtual classroom are fully installed and updated on all my primary and back-up computers.

☐ All my devices, back-up devices, and tech accessories are powered on and ready to go prior to the start of my hybrid class.

☐ All my devices, back-up devices, and tech accessories are fully charged and can run from battery power if needed.

Subtotal: _____

Hybrid Classroom Technology

☐ I know the full extent of the capabilities that my hybrid classroom technology has.

☐ When connected as the host, I know what every button and every menu command does.

☐ When connected as a participant, I know what every button and every menu command does.

☐ I am aware of all unique features of my hybrid classroom technology (e.g., how to establish audio connections without echo, how to enable webcams, how to use breakouts, etc.).

☐ I know how to share screens, documents, and other files using the hybrid classroom technology and/or virtual classroom software.

☐ I have tested every feature and activity that we will be using in the hybrid class.

Subtotal: _____

If the Facilitator Is Remote

- ☐ I have a reliable computer or laptop that I can use to facilitate the hybrid class.
- ☐ I have a second reliable laptop or mobile device that I can use as a backup to facilitate hybrid classes.
- ☐ I have a solid high-speed internet connection in the location where I will be facilitating the hybrid class.
- ☐ I have a back-up internet connection in the location where I will be facilitating the hybrid class.
- ☐ I have established a way to reach participants in case of internet connectivity issues.
- ☐ I have selected an in-room moderator who will assist throughout the program.
- ☐ I will use an external microphone or a quality headset to ensure a clear audio connection.
- ☐ I have a back-up audio connection that can be used if needed (e.g., my main connection is VoIP and my back-up connection is a mobile phone).
- ☐ My primary headset is fully charged prior to the start of the event.
- ☐ My backup audio devices are all fully charged prior to the start of the event.

Subtotal: _____

Facilitator and Participant Technology Support

- ☐ I have an assigned producer who will assist with all technology needs during the hybrid class.
- ☐ I have a back-up producer who could fill in for the producer if needed.
- ☐ I have another facilitator who could fill in for me at the last minute if needed.
- ☐ I have a technology specialist available to assist remote participants behind the scenes.
- ☐ I have arranged for another technical support person who knows how to use the hybrid technology to be on call in case of tech difficulties.

Subtotal: _____

Audio/Video/Technology

- ☐ The hybrid classroom has capability for quality audio connections during the event. All co-located participants will be clearly heard.
- ☐ Remote participants have instructions and support to have clearly heard audio.
- ☐ The hybrid classroom has a camera setup where all participants can be easily seen.
- ☐ Remote participants have instruction and support to use webcams during the hybrid learning experience.
- ☐ Audio and video guidelines have been (or will be) established by the beginning of the hybrid class (i.e., when to use mute, when to be on camera).
- ☐ All participants, regardless of location, will connect to the virtual classroom platform using a device so they have equal access to the tools.

Subtotal: _____

Activities and Materials

- ☐ All planned activities (polls, whiteboards, breakouts, etc.) have been tested and are ready to use during the hybrid class.
- ☐ The facilitator has a copy of every document associated with the hybrid event (e.g., facilitator guide, participant materials).
- ☐ Participants have (or will have easy access to) a copy of all participant materials associated with the hybrid event (e.g., job aids, activity instructions).

Subtotal: _____

Participants and Learning Transfer

- ☐ I know the participants' names and job roles prior to the hybrid class.
- ☐ I know the length of time participants have been with their organization.
- ☐ I know the participants' biggest challenges related to the training topic.
- ☐ I know how participants need to apply the learning back on the job.
- ☐ I have anticipated the questions that participants will have related to the training topic.

- [ ] I have verified that participants have completed all prerequisites or pre-session assignments for the training topic.
- [ ] I know whether participants have talked with their direct supervisor about the application of the learning.
- [ ] I know the business/organizational results expected by stakeholders as a result of this hybrid learning experience.

Subtotal: _____

Grand Total: _____

Scoring Key

50   Perfect score! Enter your name on the Extra-Prepared Hybrid Facilitator All-Star List!

45–49   Excellent! Consider helping other facilitators learn from your efforts.

35–44   Congratulations! You are prepared to deliver hybrid learning experiences.

25–34   You may be prepared but have room for improvement. Select a few areas where you can extend your preparation.

15–24   You are on the verge of preparation. Identify at least five items you can add to your hybrid delivery preparation.

0–14   Go through the recommendations in this chapter, and ask an experienced hybrid facilitator for assistance in getting started.

CHAPTER 5

Facilitating Blended Learning Journeys

Think back to the last time you mastered a challenging new skill. What was it and how did you learn it? If it was a complex skill, and if you're like most people, you likely didn't learn it in a day. You probably learned it over time, with practice. You may have taken a class, worked with a mentor, or spent time perfecting the technique. Or maybe you searched for information on the internet, watched a demonstration, and then tried it on your own.

However you did it, and however long it took, your learning journey probably included several different sources. This is what we call a blended experience.

What's in a Name? Blended, Journey, Hybrid, and More

To be clear, in our context, *blended* refers to *a learning process with multiple cohesive components taking place over a designated period of time.* It may involve self-study, peer group collaboration, demonstrations, facilitator-led classes, or any other method deemed necessary to learn that skill. It's not a random set of jumbled experiences (although it's possible to learn that way too), but instead it's *a thoughtfully planned set of experiences designed to help you learn.*

A blended learning experience could consist of all asynchronous assignments, or it could be a series of synchronous gatherings. But it's usually an intentional combination of both. Note that while it's also possible for the journey to be a fully individual endeavor, typically it's experienced with others.

The most common type of blended learning journey assigns participants to a cohort, following along a prescribed series of learning opportunities, with a designated start and stop date. See Figure 5-1 for an example of an eight-week blended learning journey.

FIGURE 5-1. A Sample Blended Learning Journey

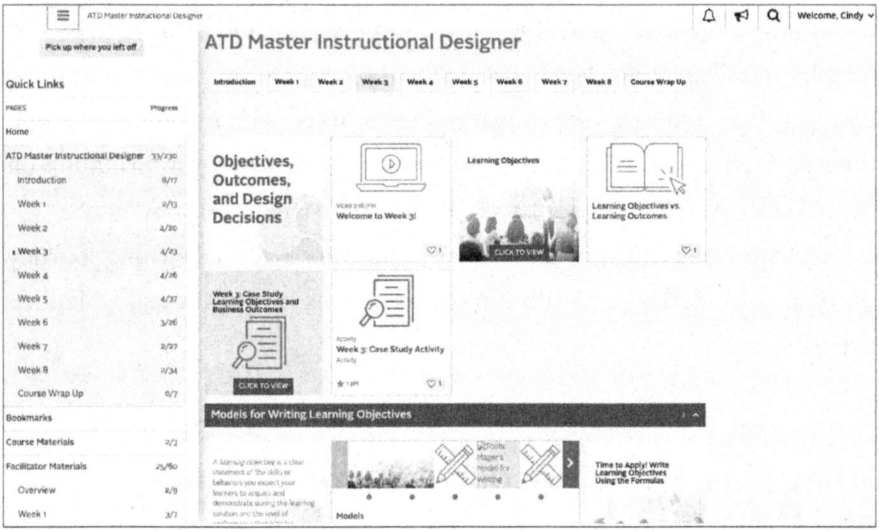

For example, I recently took a marketing class for small-business owners that was created to be a blended journey. My cohort began on the first day of the month, when we gained access to the online portal. The first set of assignments was asynchronous—a collection of worksheets designed to help us determine our learning goals and explore the program's many references and resources. We then met online with the facilitator, who provided a program overview and answered our questions. Over the next several weeks, we completed a variety of activities, including reading, watching videos, completing tasks, and meeting with the facilitator. By the end of the program, I achieved my learning goals—a marketing plan created with input from my peers and expert guidance from the facilitator. It was a well-planned and well-designed learning experience.

The other descriptive term, *journey*, aptly describes the idea that blended learning is a process that takes time. It's rarely a linear straight shot, but instead a meandering method of absorbing, practicing, reflecting, and learning.

It's also important to be clear that *blended* does not mean the same thing as *hybrid*, even though some organizations do use *hybrid* in place of *blended*. As noted in the previous chapter, this definition is perpetuated by the "hybrid courses" offered by many universities, which have multiple components— some asynchronous (like reading and studying) and some synchronous (like classroom lectures). However, in the corporate world, this same course structure is called *blended*.

In workplace learning, *hybrid* simply refers to a mixed-location audience in a facilitator-led class. Some participants are in person while others join in remotely. See the previous chapter for more about facilitating hybrid classes.

Another term commonly confused with blended learning is the *flipped classroom*, which has roots in the K–12 environment. Instead of going to class to listen to lectures and then doing homework problems at home, flipped classroom students do the opposite. They watch a video lecture at home to learn the concepts, and then work the problems during class when the teacher is available to help and answer questions. This idea is similar to a blended learning journey because it includes both asynchronous and synchronous components.

Although my preferred term for this type of learning is the *blended learning journey*, there are many other variations. It's also been called a *guided learning journey*, a *learning campaign*, and a *learning path*. In addition, some technology vendors have their own proprietary names, such as Robert Brinkerhoff's High-Impact Learning Journey.

While there are slight nuances between these definitions, it's not enough to distinguish them as separate entities. And the facilitator role is similar enough in all of them that we can group them together.

A Blended Journey as an Immersive Learning Experience

How does a blended learning journey qualify as an immersive experience? First, we typically think of "immersive" in terms of the participant getting absorbed into a realistic but artificially created virtual environment. A well-designed blended learning journey does the inverse, but with the same effect. Instead of removing the participant from their surroundings and placing them into an artificial one, the blended journey is embedded into the participant's world. In other words, the learning components are baked into their workweek through assignments and activities. From that perspective, it is an immersive experience.

A blended learning journey may also include immersive components. For example, participants could be asked to complete a virtual reality assignment or use augmented reality resources. Or they may go through a series of self-led assignments, meet with the facilitator in a virtual classroom, and then jump into a virtual simulation for practice and feedback. The design possibilities are endless.

Finally, blended learning journeys are a relatively recent addition to most organizational learning initiatives. Blended learning isn't new, but it has changed in recent years. Digital platforms, mobile devices, better internet bandwidth, and other technologies are now mainstream. Many of these technologies are immersive in nature and have led to new tools for engagement, involvement, and learning.

Whether your blended learning journeys are immersive or more traditional, they are likely saturated with newer technologies. With the increased adoption of technology-based learning comes new expectations and skills for facilitators. Learning experience facilitators need to be well versed in all modern learning methods, including blended learning journeys.

The Benefits of Blended Learning

Before diving into the facilitator's role in the blended learning journey, we need to first address why a facilitator is needed. To do that, consider both the benefits and challenges of this learning method. These insights will set the stage for the skills facilitators need to enable and support immersive participant learning.

There are numerous benefits of blended learning. Participants in a blended learning journey:

- ► Can learn largely on their own time, according to their own schedule
- ► Can practice new skills in their current setting with realistic dynamics
- ► Have built-in reflection time between components
- ► Have access to an expert facilitator when needed, plus the opportunity to learn with like-minded peers

Assuming the program is well designed, participants will walk away being able to apply their new skills on the job. Let's take a closer look at two of the more notable benefits: time-saving and practice.

Time-Saving Efficiencies

Most people think that blended learning saves time. And while that's partially true, it's not the full truth. In my conversations with instructional designers who have converted in-person programs to blended learning, a large number have shared that they were able to shave time by eliminating content. That makes me wonder why the content was included in the first place. And, if that eliminated content was important, how will the participants learn it now? What's the job impact of omitting those details?

In general, the overall amount of learning time in a blended journey should be close to the same as that of an in-person workshop. In other words, a 14-hour class converted to a blended curriculum will likely require about 14 hours to complete. For example, in the classroom version of my Virtual Facilitation Skills program, we begin at 8:30 a.m. and finish at 4:30 p.m. Removing lunch and breaks, it's about a seven-hour program. In the program's blended format, we begin with a short, 30-minute online orientation, after which participants leave with their first assignment. We meet three more times (90 minutes each) in the virtual classroom, and participants complete assignments between each gathering. The overall curriculum still takes about seven hours to complete.

The time-saving efficiencies of blended learning come from other areas besides learning time (or "seat time," as we used to call it). Participants aren't leaving their desks for large swaths of time, and travel time to and from the workshop location is eliminated too. And blended components are typically designed in shorter chunks, resulting in a more efficient learning experience.

Most blended programs have more asynchronous components than their fully in-person counterparts, which allows participants to set their own schedules for learning. In a recent blended program I participated in, I watched the short asynchronous video components while on the treadmill at the gym. It was a huge time-saver for me because I completed my daily workout and learning tasks at the same time, something that couldn't have been replicated if it was an in-person program.

The efficiency of blended learning journeys recognizes the current reality of adult learners who are often overwhelmed and overworked. Why bring them together at a set time that's convenient for the facilitator but not necessarily the participant? Instead, participants have the flexibility to learn on their own time, on their own schedule, and at their own convenience.

FULLY ASYNCHRONOUS BLENDED LEARNING JOURNEYS?

It's possible for a blended journey to be completely asynchronous, and even in this format, a facilitator adds value. For example, ATD's Master Instructional Designer program is an eight-week asynchronous blended learning journey.

Participants receive weekly assignments, work through case studies, post in discussion board threads, take knowledge assessments, and submit a design project for evaluation. Every aspect of the program is self-led, with no virtual meetings or other synchronous events.

As a facilitator of this blended program, I greet participants and serve as the resident expert and host. I post reminders, monitor progress, respond to questions, and encourage participation. I also provide feedback, supplement the content with my own experience and resources, and help everyone make connections between the content and its application in the real world. Finally, I "grade" the design projects against a ratings rubric to help ensure mastery of the skills. My role as facilitator is to guide and support the participants during their learning journey.

Practicing New Skills

Another key benefit of blended learning is its ability to provide real-world practice exercises throughout the journey. Because participants stay in their workplace for the experience, they are surrounded by everyday situations. This means that, depending on the training topic, they likely have ample opportunities to try out their new skills.

Practice opportunities in a blended learning journey have two distinct advantages. First is the superior quality of the practice experience. It's common in the traditional classroom to provide rehearsal opportunities through role plays or other simulations. Unfortunately, these fabricated practices just can't compete with the real thing. They depend upon the quality of the simulation design, along with the acting abilities of the other participants. The opportunity to interact and practice with real customers or real recipients, on the other hand, can be a game-changer for learning new skills.

Another advantage of practice opportunities in the blended journey is the timing. Most traditional training events occur in a formal classroom, and participants may or may not have the chance to use their new skills right away. Even in a one-day class, participants aren't back on the job until the following day.

But in a blended journey, it's much easier to include immediate, real-world practice drills on the job. The immediacy of rehearsal and application helps integrate the new skill into memory and use. For example, several years ago I worked with a hotel chain that brought its new managers together for a six-week orientation program to learn how to run a local property. However, it wasn't until returning home, several weeks after they'd learned about a topic, that participants had a true chance to apply their new knowledge. This created a significant time gap between learning and doing. When the organization decided to revamp the orientation, it turned it into a blended learning journey. The new managers stayed at their own property, spent several hours in the morning learning new content, and then worked in the business in the afternoon. Designated practice opportunities were built into the curriculum to ensure immediate rehearsal and application. It was a better learning experience for the participants and created improved results for the organization.

The Challenges of Blended Learning

Despite the many benefits of blended learning, its challenges magnify the need for facilitator involvement. In my experience, when skilled facilitators come alongside participants to support and guide them in the journey, it results in a better experience with more positive learning outcomes.

Some of the common problems with blended learning exist in any training program—for example, participants who don't have support from their direct manager, participants who have technology or access barriers, or participants who were forced to sign up for compliance or nonessential purposes. Setting aside these typical situations, there are two notable challenges that are unique to the blended format: mismatched perceptions and ongoing motivation. Let's take a closer look at each.

Mismatched Perceptions

Despite messaging that says otherwise, many participants perceive self-led learning activities as less important or even optional. When a blended program contains a combination of asynchronous assignments and synchronous live events, the live events always seem more important and are given priority. For example, if participants are assigned an article to read before coming to a facilitator-led virtual class, most will think the reading is optional, especially if the program materials call the assignment "pre-work." This incorrect assumption creates a myriad of problems, most important the lack of learning that occurs when assignments aren't completed. Facilitators are forced to waste time reviewing concepts that participants should have learned before the live event, because learners will be lost without the necessary background information.

This challenge can be overcome through proper program marketing and well-designed journeys. In addition, an active facilitator's skilled communication, guidance, and encouragement can help solve this situation.

Ongoing Motivation

I have been a part of countless blended learning journeys where participants start with excitement and then falter along the way. It happens in nearly every blended program I've designed, facilitated, or attended, for one reason or another. People have every intention of completing a learning journey, only to find that life gets in the way of completing their assignments. Many of these obstacles are justified and unavoidable—a participant gets sick, or changes roles, or gets pulled into a new, high-profile job assignment. However, when participant motivation crumbles, we have a problem that needs attention. In that situation, the learning needs to take place, but it doesn't, which means learning results won't be achieved.

As mentioned earlier, participant motivation falls into two categories: internal and external. My favorite participants in any learning program are ones who are internally motivated. They want to learn, engage, and be part of the experience. They see the benefits and potential outcomes, and they willingly join in.

Yet even internally motivated participants can get distracted and side-tracked. I've fallen into this category myself. For instance, a few years ago I signed up for a blended learning journey with a favorite facilitator, on a topic I'm passionate about. I also needed continuing education credits for a certification I hold, and it was a great fit in both content and timing. I began with enthusiasm and every good intention. And then other priorities seeped into my schedule, and I struggled mightily to complete the program. I had to ask for an extension (more than once!). It wasn't a matter of motivation; instead it became a matter of priorities.

Externally motivated participants complete blended learning journeys because of the outside influences that sway their decisions. These participants might have to complete the program for a job requirement, or perhaps built-in compulsory components (such as tests or quizzes) must be completed before they can move on. These external influences create incentives for participants to persevere.

A key facilitator skill in blended learning journeys is to encourage participants along the way: to assist them with planning and motivation. To help them see the benefits of learning and the rewards for finishing. The way the facilitator approaches this responsibility will have a direct impact on participant motivation, both internal and external.

Let's turn to the facilitator role now.

The Facilitator Role in Blended Learning Journeys

Because blended learning journeys are largely self-directed, participants have more responsibility to achieve their own learning goals. Self-motivated, disciplined participants have an advantage over those who struggle with time management and those who have competing priorities. Therefore, a skilled learning experience facilitator who expertly guides participants through the journey can mean the difference between success or failure.

In general, because of their typical format, blended learning journeys need more structure and organization than other programs. This might not seem intuitive, but with the shift of responsibility to participants, the increased number of learning components, and more moving parts overall, the administrative tasks multiply. Therefore, a facilitator in a blended learning journey takes on more than facilitators in other environments.

Two categories of facilitation tasks are required for a successful blended learning journey: **administrative tasks and learning responsibilities** (Table 5-1).

As the saying goes, "Many hands make light work." It's ideal to have a team effort supporting a blended learning journey. But ideal doesn't mean reality. Not every organization or every blended learning journey will have multiple people supporting it. I've been a one-person training department before and know from experience what it's like to wear many hats to support successful learning programs. Regardless of who actually does the tasks, they are all required for the blended journey to be successful. Table 5-1 presents a brief summary.

TABLE 5-1. Required Administrative Tasks and Learning Responsibilities for a Successful Blended Learning Journey

Administrative Tasks	Learning Responsibilities
Enrollments	Connect
Announcements	Communicate
Reminders	Coach
Escalation	Create community
Material management	Curate

Administrative Tasks

Tech tools like a learning management system (LMS) or a learning experience platform (LXP) can automate many of the administrative tasks required for a successful blended journey. These platforms can send reminders, run reports, and take care of the minutiae. The best learning systems can even personalize and adapt according to learner preference and need. For example, once a participant is enrolled in a program, they can choose how to access materials and how often they receive reminders. After an initial, one-time administrative setup, the technology takes over.

Despite the possibility of tech assistance, some administrative tasks require human involvement. And, just as it's important to learn underlying math concepts before using a calculator, it's essential to understand these clerical components of a blended learning journey before delegating them to the LMS or LXP. A task might not seem important when it's done, but it's noticeable when it's missed. For instance, if the link to a required assignment is broken, then the learners won't complete it. Also, these tasks are bare necessities for those facilitators who don't have the luxury of assistance from others or the technology support. They form the foundation and support the structure of the blended learning journey.

There are five main administrative tasks to complete: enrollments, announcements, reminders, escalation, and material management. Each task, whether completed by the facilitator or a support person, or automated through technology, enables the learning experience. It provides support *around* the learning experience so the facilitator can provide support *in* the learning experience.

Administrative Task 1: Enrollments

Whether a blended learning journey is self-selected open enrollment (that is, anyone can sign up) or required by job function, there's more to enrollment than meets the eye. The self-directed emphasis of most blended learning journeys requires participants to take on more responsibility and commitment. Therefore, getting the right people into the right programs plays a part in learning success.

When done well, enrollment can begin the immersive experience. The program description should excite and entice participants to learn. It needs to help them see the benefits of participation all the way to program completion. When participants get "hooked" from the start, they eagerly anticipate what's to come. The result is a more positive attitude about the program and an increased chance they'll take part in it.

Upon enrollment, participants should receive an overview of the entire journey with detail about what to expect. This information should outline their time commitment and responsibilities, along with any technical requirements or other important details. It should clearly communicate everything needed so that there are no surprises down the road.

I have found visually appealing checklists to be very helpful for showing participants both the high-level program information and the assignment details. See Figure 5-2 on the next page for an example.

Administrative Task 2: Announcements

Participants need to know what to do along every step of the learning journey, and when to do it. One initial announcement upon registration is rarely enough. Announcements provide vital information such as program start dates, location of learning materials, and virtual classroom links. Many people view these types of announcements as boring and mundane. But while that may be true, they also allow participation, which enables learning and engagement, which is essential for the path to completion.

The best announcements are personalized and tailored to each participant. Standard advice from email marketers says that people are more likely to open an email from a person rather than a system (White 2016). In addition, several studies show that emails with personalized subject lines are 29 percent more likely to be opened, and personalized email messages improve engagement rates (Burstein 2014). In other words, participants who feel seen are more likely to engage.

Whatever method you use to send announcements—automated or hand-typed—they contribute to the overall learning experience. Be intentional about them.

FIGURE 5-2. Sample Blended Learning Journey Participant Checklist

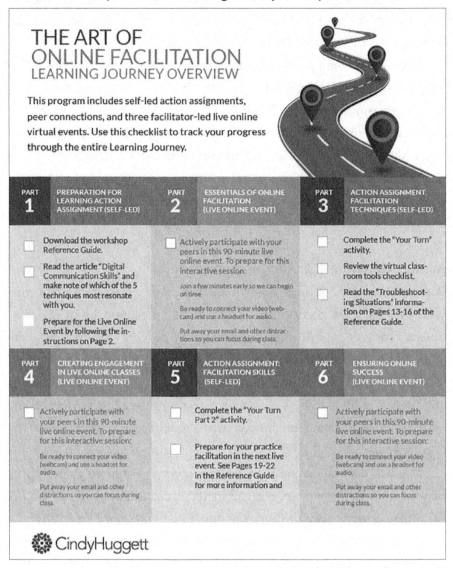

Administrative Task 3: Reminders

Reminders are similar to announcements in a blended learning journey, seen as just a necessary part of the program. However, they are often the difference between a participant finishing the journey or starting and then stalling. In our overworked, overscheduled, oversaturated world, participants need reminders. And some need them more than others. They need reminders sent at just the right time, with just the right tone. There's a fine balance between nagging and reminding, so it's important to err on the side of gentle nudging.

In a six-week blended learning journey, with weekly assignments and virtual classes, reminders could be sent at the beginning of each week as well as the morning of each facilitator-led event. Then, if there's a final assignment to complete, a reminder about it would also be helpful.

We'll cover more specifics about communication techniques in the next section. For now, recognize the importance of reminders in the program flow of blended learning journeys.

VOICES FROM THE FIELD

"How do you keep participants motivated in a blended learning journey? This is a tough question; life gets busy, and people have a hard time prioritizing self-directed work. Keep it simple, make sure your directions are complete and clear, and send timely reminders. Never assume that learners can find assignments you've sent previously. When you send a reminder, include a link or attach materials so that the learner doesn't have to go hunting to find the assignment again."
—**Maureen Orey, Founder and CEO, Workplace Learning and Performance Group**

Administrative Task 4: Escalation

Immersive blended learning journeys require commitment and discipline. Despite the best starting intentions, participants may get behind on assignment completion or disappear from the program altogether. Sometimes they have valid reasons like job changes or emergencies. But if their absence is a result of poor planning or lack of motivation, then external influence may be required.

First, prepare in advance for this possibility by creating an escalation plan. Decide what will be done and by whom when a participant falls behind the planned schedule. Does the LMS or LXP track participation and send out automated reminders when something isn't completed? Or is it the facilitator's responsibility to monitor progress and reach out to participants who are lagging behind? Of course, it's possible that the learning journey has no time limits or consequences for dropping out—in that case nothing will be done. Or maybe you show grace in the moment, with understanding that things happen and offer the option to switch to a future cohort on a better time schedule.

Some designers will build options into the journey, such as an advance determination that a program is completed once a certain number of components are finished. For example, they might create a series of six virtual classes with follow-on assignments for each and note that it's OK if a participant misses one of the six classes. There's inherent danger in that approach because it may reinforce the notion that the learning experience doesn't have to be a top priority. But for some roles, some programs, and some organizations, setting an 80 to 90 percent completion target may be sufficient.

Another option is to structure the journey with discretionary-but-encouraged assignments. For example, I facilitate a blended learning journey that has four bi-weekly assignments, each with a designated due date. There's incentive to complete the assignments on time because they'll get feedback from their colleagues and time to revise before the final program date if they do. However, as long as participants complete all four assignments by the end of the journey, they are credited with completion—there's no penalty for falling behind.

If job requirements or other factors dictate that participants must complete a program, but participants don't respond to reminders, an escalation sequence should begin. If they're not completing program assignments due to their workload, then involve their direct manager in the conversation (Figure 5-3). The manager may need to step in, either to help reorganize priorities or provide another level of motivation for completion. If the participants aren't employees, the escalation sequence may need to refer back to the participant contract or program agreement (assuming one was built into the program!).

Escalations are not usually fun for facilitators or participants. Facilitators may want to avoid confrontation, and participants don't want to hear bad news. At the same time, an escalation-based extra nudge may be all that's needed to add incentive for learning.

FIGURE 5-3. Sample Escalation Message

[Manager name],

You are receiving this message because your associate [Learner's name] is part of the current [program name] cohort.

We regret to inform you that so far, they have not yet completed the required assignments and they missed the first live online class that is part of their assignment to [program name].

Because they are quite late, we are now requesting them to urgently catch up on the assignment and prepare to attend the next live online class. We will check in on them again tomorrow.

If they still do not confirm their participation in the above events by Thursday, regrettably we would then be required to remove them from the program.

Should you have any questions or comments, feel free to contact me.

Kind regards,
[Name]

Administrative Task 5: Material Management

The final administrative task is to manage the program materials, which include participant e-books, facilitator guides, ancillary documents, and anything else that helps the program run smoothly. There may also be tangible items to inventory and distribute, like manuals, hands-on equipment, or even VR headsets (if VR is built into the journey). This step involves getting materials posted online or delivered to the right location.

Posting online materials to an LMS, LXP, or another electronic repository may be a one-time task or it could be an ongoing responsibility. For example, some platforms require a fresh post for each new cohort prior to the start of their journey. And for physical items, these likely need to be shipped every time.

You may also need to provide an element of material version control for the program to run smoothly. For example, if AR markers are embedded into participant materials, they may need to be checked periodically to ensure they are still active. Or if virtual classroom links are posted, these may need to be updated with each new cohort.

This list of administrative tasks may seem quite transactional in nature. Yet they are essential elements for a successful blended learning journey. Not every organization has the luxury of learning coordinators or other administrative roles, so these responsibilities often fall to the facilitator, who does them on top of their learning role. Now let's turn our attention to the second category of items—the learning responsibilities.

BUILDING A BUSINESS CASE FOR ADMINISTRATIVE SUPPORT

Several years ago, I partnered with a large global manufacturer to help it create a successful strategy for its blended learning journeys. We calculated the estimated amount of time needed to fully support each journey. Then we split apart the administrative and facilitator tasks to determine how many hours fell into each category. Finally, we totaled the number of people per cohort, and the expected number of cohorts per year.

By taking the time to calculate these data points, we were able to build the business case for administrative support. Our recommendation was approved with overwhelming support because the numbers were clear.

Learning Responsibilities

A skilled facilitator can make or break the learning experience for participants in their blended journey. They are the tour guide, feedback provider, question asker, discussion board monitor, expert instructor, and encouraging cheerleader all in one. Their purpose is to help participants learn and apply the content, and they lead the blended learning journey, shepherding participants along the path.

Because every journey is different, the facilitator's role will vary accordingly. In one journey, for example, the facilitator may play an active role in discussion board postings as well as leading the live events (in person, virtual, or both). In another journey, the facilitator may act as a coach who meets individually with each participant to help them process the learning experience. The responsibilities listed here are common considerations for learning and transcend all program designs.

In my first manager role, I was told that my job was to help my team "between the white spaces" on the company org chart. This meant that it was my responsibility to help my team navigate relationships and responsibilities to get the job done. They controlled their own tasks; I was just the thread that helped link things together.

This same description holds true for learning experience facilitators in blended journeys. Participants have a set of learning activities to complete and it's their responsibility to do it. The facilitator is simply there to guide and assist.

The five main learning responsibilities—connect, communicate, coach, create community, and curate—are completed by the facilitator who directly supports the participant experience. Note that these actions are specific to blended learning journeys. If the curriculum includes virtual classes, hybrid events, or VR simulations, then refer to the facilitator skills that are covered in the corresponding chapters.

Learning Responsibility 1: Connect

The first way facilitators connect in a learning journey is by building rapport and relationships with participants. In doing so, they personalize the learning experience, become the face of the program, set the tone, and provide a sense of comfort for participants who want to know they are in good hands for the experience.

Another way facilitators connect during a journey is to help participants learn. Skilled facilitators help participants connect the learning content to the real world. They provide context for scenarios and situations that the learners may encounter on the job, and share relevant stories out of their own experience to bring the content to life. For example, a new manager learning about empathy may wonder when they would use that skill, and subconsciously discount its importance. But they realize the relevance after reading the facilitator's discussion board post about a time when they successfully used an empathetic response with an employee.

The actual technique of connecting will vary from program to program, depending upon its structure. In a blended learning journey that I facilitate, the first component is a virtual class, during which we take time to get to know one another. In another blended learning journey, we begin by posting on discussion boards, so I upload a welcome video where I establish program expectations and set the tone for participation (Figure 5-4). And in still another journey, I send a personalized welcome note to each participant as a way to begin a conversation with them. Determine the method that works best for your situation.

FIGURE 5-4.
Sample Facilitator Welcome Message for a Blended Learning Journey

Learning Responsibility 2: Communicate

A facilitator who performs the program's administrative tasks will have ample opportunity to communicate with participants, because they'll be sending reminders throughout the journey. On the other hand, facilitators who partner with others will need to scope out opportunities to communicate with participants at appropriate program touchpoints.

Communication may be the single most important facilitation skill in a blended learning journey. These online programs need more structure and interactions to help compensate for the self-directed journey. When participants are left alone, they may wonder if they're on track or may get lost along the way. But participants who receive timely communications at appropriate times will be more likely to thrive and learn.

Communication could be largely limited to asynchronous methods, where facilitators post questions and respond to comments. Or it could be active discussion during synchronous events. Either way, the facilitator's tone should be positive and uplifting. It should serve to enhance the learning. In addition, this is a good opportunity to model excellent interpersonal skills by providing clear instructions and easy-to-read text.

One of my favorite facilitators is someone I've never met in person. She led a short asynchronous blended learning journey I participated in, and her personality shone through in her posts. They weren't about her; she kept the focus on the learners. But she shared just enough of herself that I felt like she was real and relatable. For instance, she would briefly mention that she was sipping a cup of tea while writing a response. Or share that one of our discussion board conversations reminded her of a prior similar experience. It was just enough to give a glimpse into her world, as she was helping us navigate ours.

Learning Responsibility 3: Coach

There can be a fine line between a coach and a critic. The best facilitators act as coaches during a learning experience by providing feedback in ways that encourage participants to continue along the journey. Coaches bring out the best in people through insightful questions that point people in the right direction.

In a blended learning journey, facilitators do the same. They pose discussion and reflection questions. They help learners see what's possible and lead them there, giving gentle guidance and strong support along the way.

If the journey includes practice opportunities or more formal assessments, the facilitator can either directly provide feedback or help the learner process feedback they receive from other sources.

Recently I needed to coach a participant in one of my blended learning journeys who had missed the mark on her first two assignments. She was falling behind the rest of the cohort and the tone of her discussion board posts indicated confusion. It was clear that she needed some extra assistance. After a few email exchanges didn't fully resolve the issue, we had several one-on-one phone conversations. My questions and our resulting conversations helped her discover the source of her challenges. She had misunderstood the assignment expectations, and had less experience than the rest of the group. As a result, she needed more explanations and additional content resources. Ultimately, we were able to sort through the issues and get her back on track.

Learning Responsibility 4: Create Community

A significant participant success factor in most types of cohort-based online learning is a sense of shared community. This is true in stand-alone virtual classes as well as blended learning journeys. Because participants are physically separated from one another, connected only in digital spaces, they may feel isolated and alone. Motivation may wane during the learning experience if they think they are on their own.

Traditional learning programs have three directions of conversation:

- ▶ Trainer to participant is when the facilitator teaches content.
- ▶ Participant to trainer is when participants respond to the facilitator's questions.
- ▶ Participant to participant happens when participants work in small groups for program activities.

Effective facilitators emphasize the participant-to-participant connection in blended learning journeys. The group can learn from and encourage one another. This helps create accountability when working together on shared projects or interests.

Facilitators create community when they help participants connect in meaningful ways. For example, if a participant asks a question, and the facilitator knows that another participant has experience in that area, they can encourage conversation between them. Or, the facilitator might intentionally assign subgroups or partners among the cohort based on location or job function.

In my experience, participants who feel like they belong in the community will be more likely to engage in activities, contribute to discussions, and complete their journey.

VOICES FROM THE FIELD

"My best strategy for the in-between is to have 'buddies' (or accountability partners) who set an appointment to work together on the assignment and be ready to present at the next session." —**Nanci Appleman-Vassil, Founder and CEO, APLS Group**

Learning Responsibility 5: Curate

An expert facilitator curates topical content that's tailored to participants in the learning journey. They bring in external sources to enhance the learning program. Like a museum curator, they carefully select the most relevant pieces that add value to the experience.

For instance, let's say a facilitator discovers that many of the customer service reps in a new-hire orientation journey came from a competitor's organization, and therefore already have experience with a similar customer relationship management platform. The facilitator could include a chart comparing their old platform with the new platform, which would allow the group to more quickly learn how to use it. This curated content isn't usually part of the learning experience, but it adds value for this specific group. While curated content may seem out of context, it's the special touch that a skilled facilitator can provide to personalize and enhance the blended learning journey.

CASE STUDY The Facilitator's Role in Blended Learning

An interview with Carrie Addington, Senior Manager of Learning Experience and Facilitator Development, Association for Talent Development

Since it was introduced in 2012, ATD's Master Trainer® Program has been the go-to for professionals looking to validate their training delivery skills. When it was launched, the program was divided into four distinct parts:

1. A self-directed online orientation
2. An in-person four-day core course
3. A supplemental elective course
4. A wrap-up assignment

It was assessment-based, which means participants needed to pass both a knowledge exam and a skills demonstration to earn their Master Trainer designation.

For the Master Trainer facilitators, all their energy was focused on teaching the in-person core course. Their involvement in part one was limited to a welcome message and a few discussion board posts, and participants completed the elective and wrap-up independently.

The program was recently updated, and is now offered as a blended program through ATD's online learning platform with facilitator-led sessions. It remains assessment-based with a focus on opportunities to demonstrate skills, but has been reformatted as an eight-week guided learning journey. As a result, the facilitator's role has also changed.

Facilitators are now active for the entire duration of the program, helping learners link course components for increased retention when they are back in their daily workflow. The facilitator's asynchronous interactions include leading meaningful interactions to connect participants with one another and the information; reading between the lines in participant comments, posts, and assignments; and providing expert guidance by sharing examples and stories to help ground the content in practical application.

The Master Trainer Program is a guided learning journey, which makes the facilitators' practical expertise a key part of the course experience and vital to the integrity of the ATD brand. As well as assessing and developing participants' training delivery skills and providing individualized feedback on assignments, facilitators also encourage participation in virtual classroom activities, discussions, and breakout sessions.

"The program leverages a new platform, a new learning experience, and updated content aligned to the Talent Development Capability Model," explains Carrie Addington, senior manager of learning experience and facilitator development at ATD. "The facilitator's role is to synthesize these components into an engaging learning experience."

To help participants and facilitators transition to a more self-directed and technology-reliant program, ATD also created a temporary learning experience support role, the ATD Masters Concierge.

"They addressed difficulties with the technology that might prevent participants from fully engaging with the learning experience," Carrie says. "With multiple technology systems and a diverse set of program components and requirements, we wanted to provide the necessary support to optimize the participants' engagement and success in the program."

There was a clear delineation between the facilitator and the concierge. Whereas the concierge was on hand to solve any technical challenges, anything pertaining to learning objectives or program outcomes was directed to the program facilitator.

Delivering this type of dynamic, blended learning program requires a significant shift in mindset for the facilitators. It's not simply a case of transitioning face-to-face training skills to an online platform.

"You have to be intentional with your facilitation," Carrie explains. "In a blended program this means being detailed and frequent with communications, knowing that participants will need a guide to usher them through the key components of the blend and help them connect those concepts to their daily work. It also means linking content in different modalities to help participants see how the content in an asynchronous portion informs an activity that is being conducted in the live online or face-to-face portion."

The program's element of peer-to-peer collaboration has also affected the facilitator's role. Rather than always leading the discussion, facilitators often just step back and observe. "It takes a lot of restraint to stop yourself from getting in there," Carrie says. "You have to say to yourself: 'The learners are having the conversation; the learning is taking place and I'm not needed at this point.' And that's a shift in mindset because we're so used to facilitating every conversation."

Clearly, the ATD Master Trainer Program requires master-level facilitators who are consistently modeling the elevated training delivery skills that the program teaches. They are responsible for guiding learners through practical application, providing expert guidance and relevant examples, allowing for personalized learning through case studies and scenarios, and fostering peer-to-peer collaboration.

"To ensure performance, we supported facilitators by providing structured curriculum materials that were predesigned to provide the necessary instructions, prompts, guidance, and rubrics to ensure clarity and consistency for the facilitator," Carrie says. "When developing facilitator materials for this program, we tried to think of everything a facilitator could possibly need—from tracking sheets to templates and communications—to streamline the preparation process and enable facilitators to link content pieces together for learners. There's a lot of 'Here's what good feedback looks like and the tools to get you there,' so facilitators aren't left to create tools and templates for the program's success on their own."

Keeping pace with a new way of working is a challenge for any facilitator, so what's Carrie's top tip for embracing change?

"When it comes to preparing for a blended program," she advises, "engage with the different technologies and platforms to understand the learner's experience. I move through the program as the learner would and interact with the technologies as if I'm a learner. This allows me to anticipate their needs and provide more guidance in moments of the program that are more layered. I also spend a lot of time preparing for how I'll strategically link the modalities together to increase retention and engagement. The most important role we play in a blend is to connect the content that is covered asynchronously with a discussion or activity that is experienced in the live online or face-to-face classroom."

"When it comes to embracing change, I try to find what makes me uncomfortable and go after that," she continues. "I want to become knowledgeable—find experts, seek out articles, read widely, and talk to colleagues. Because that's the fun part, right? Nothing is static."

In today's rapidly changing business environment, that's excellent advice.

In Summary

Blended learning combines exploration and discovery with facilitated expertise. It creates more opportunities for participants to apply learning on the job. The combination of administrative tasks and learning responsibilities gives facilitators the guidance they need to successfully support learning and application. Most blended journeys benefit from facilitator support.

In the next chapter, we'll look at how facilitators can incorporate AR into the learning experience, including a blended curriculum.

Checklist: Defined Roles for a Successful Blended Learning Journey

Use this list to determine who in the organization will handle each task and responsibility.

Tasks and Responsibilities	Who Will Complete This Task?
Administrative Tasks	
Enrollments	
Announcements	
Reminders	
Escalation	
Material management	
Learning Responsibilities	
Connect	
Communicate	
Coach	
Create community	
Curate	

CHAPTER 6

Facilitating With Augmented Reality

Augmented reality (AR) has slowly creeped into our everyday lives. From social media filters to online shopping experiences, it's increasingly common to see and interact with AR objects in the midst of routine transactions. If you're using an internet-connected device for work—or for anything—you've likely noticed this trend. AR is behind the explosion of digital overlays in online meetings and 3-D images that come to life on a screen.

Therefore, it should be no surprise that AR is also seeping into training programs. From augmented virtual backgrounds when teaching online classes to using 3-D holographic models to explain how something works, these technology-driven components are gaining popularity and becoming commonplace in the classroom. So how should learning experience facilitators respond to this new technology, and how can they use it effectively? In this chapter, we'll explore the uses of AR in training programs and more importantly, the skills facilitators need to use it well.

Defining Augmented Reality

To set the stage for this conversation, let's continue the detailed explanation started in chapter 2. Remember, augmented reality consists of digital elements superimposed onto the real world. It may be simple and subtle, like closed-captioned words at the bottom of a screen. Or it could be super obvious, such as the overlay of a large object in a room (like seeing how a new bookcase would look next to the desk in your home office when shopping for furniture online). Instead of imagining an object in your mind, AR allows you to actually see it in your environment. The possibilities AR can bring to a learning environment are endless.

One reason for AR's increasing popularity is that, unlike VR, it doesn't require expensive or complicated equipment. AR uses smartphones, tablets, and other internet-connected wearables (like smartglasses and watches) that are already common in workplace settings. This means that AR can easily be added to a learning experience.

An important thing to remember about AR is that the digital components need to be activated before they can be visible onscreen. In other words, they need to be triggered. The two most common types of triggers are marker-based and markerless. Additionally, location-based AR is a subset of the markerless trigger.

> **Marker-based AR** appears when you hover a viewing device over a special image that has a digital trigger embedded into it (Figure 6-1). For example, when I take my son to our local LEGO store, he can hold any of the boxes up to a special viewing device on the wall, and it brings the model to life in 3-D. He loves watching the minifigures move around and gets ideas for how he will play with the set when

FIGURE 6-1. Example of a Marker-Based AR Experience

we get home. This would be the type of AR most commonly used in participant materials like workbooks or other handouts.

> **Markerless AR** is not launched by a trigger image. Instead, this type of AR uses location and mapping tools to bring digital objects into a physical space. This is the type of AR online shopping sites use when they prompt you to "view this item in your home." The app scans your environment (maps it) for a surface that you can "set" the item on. The objects can be moved around, and they become a digital part of the environment. In a training example, participants in a safety class on confined space entry could examine the insides of a life-size container to more easily recognize and apply the concepts learned.

▶ **Location-based AR** is a specific type of markerless AR that makes use of beacons, GPS data, and a digital compass. Your device's location triggers the AR experience instead of the point-and-click method needed for other types. For instance, in the confined space safety program, a participant could use AR to see designated escape paths based upon their current location. The popular game *Pokémon Go* may be the most well-known example of location-based AR.

Any of these types of AR can successfully be incorporated into a learning experience. Each has unique features and benefits. As a facilitator, it's helpful to know the differences between them so that you can explain them to others and use them effectively.

HOLOGRAMS FOR LEARNING

A hologram is a 3-D digital image that uses light reflection to appear real. In other words, it's a digital photo that comes to life in front of your eyes. A unique form of AR, holograms create extremely realistic digital avatars—they're like a combination of a high-resolution photo and a physical but transparent ghost.

The potential use of holograms in learning experiences is an exciting development. A subject matter expert could join a class discussion in hologram form from a remote location, and it would be like they were in the room. Or a dispersed group of global executives could come together for a brainstorming session. Going beyond video screens, holograms add in a feeling of presence.

Stay tuned to vendor announcements about burgeoning holographic technology for learning environments. For example, Cisco Webex announced in 2021 that it was piloting Webex Hologram to integrate holograms into the virtual training platform. They describe it as "a real-time, photorealistic holographic interaction that goes beyond video conferencing for a truly immersive experience" (Cisco nd). Incorporating this type of augmented reality into the virtual classroom will add an incredible new dimension to conversation and collaboration.

Now let's explore ways augmented reality can be used to enhance learning experiences.

Benefits of AR in Learning

Augmented reality adds a unique spin to learning opportunities. In addition to enhancing the real world, AR also removes traditional constraints by allowing our imagination to go to new places and broadening our minds to see what's possible. In the real world, a table touches the floor, but in a digital world, a table can float or move in unique ways. Participants can explore content from a new perspective, either up close through a magnified digital model, or from far away with an otherwise impossible bird's eye view.

Thinking about this potential in the context of learning, it brings experiences into the classroom that wouldn't otherwise be feasible or accessible. For example, AR allows you to animate participant materials or insert digital objects into otherwise static lessons, making them instantly dynamic. It's difficult to place boundaries on what it can do to enhance a learning program because the possibilities are so vast.

Like all new technologies, AR may seem appealing because it's new and different. But as we know from many other new technologies that have launched with fanfare and then faded into obscurity, "shiny object syndrome" isn't a valid reason to use AR for learning. The only acceptable reason to add digital objects to training experiences is to create value by helping participants learn. AR is a useful tool only if it contributes to achieving learning outcomes.

So, before we get carried away by the novelty, let's look at *why* using AR for learning is effective and then take a deeper dive into the *how*.

AR's first, biggest benefit for learning is its ability to simplify complex topics. It's one thing to see a photo on a slide; it's another thing to see that object come to life in front of you. A facilitator who needs to describe how something works can say, "Let's look inside to see the details," and then have participants launch an AR experience to follow along with the explanation.

For example, an electrical engineer could be looking at a digital replica of a circuit box while learning how to wire specialty fuses. Or a medical student could see the inside of a person's torso, with all its intricate details, while learning about surgery techniques. Seeing these items as if they were real creates an experience that might otherwise be impossible and enhances the learning.

Next, AR can also make something easier to understand because it allows the learner to see it in context. For example, a facilitator could use a magnified AR object to show a chemical reaction up close to a group of R&D scientists learning more about new products coming to market. Or a manufacturing facility operator could learn how to better care for equipment by seeing an up-close version of its internal workings.

Finally, AR helps create immersive learning experiences by getting participants out of their seats and into their environments. As they interact with AR components, they are drawn into the learning. AR can capture their interest in ways that static information doesn't. It can draw them deeply into the content, which is a hallmark of immersive learning. At least one study found increased participant motivation when using AR in a learning experience (Khan, Johnston, and Ophoff 2019).

Ultimately, AR adds value to a training program when it increases participant engagement to help them learn and apply the new content.

Evolution of AR in Learning Programs

As digital tools move into learning programs, it's important to remember that most traditional classroom trainers have historically used a variety of analog tools to assist with learning. From props to visual aids to tchotchkes, these items add another dimension to the in-person classroom, and they allow participants to have a more hands-on experience. For example, a facilitator might demonstrate the interconnectedness between business units to new hires using a braid of yarn. The enhanced visual demonstrates the concept and makes it easier to learn.

In a time-management class I used to facilitate, the vendor's participant kits included a folding cardboard pyramid with key concepts printed on it. Participants worked with the shape during the workshop activities, and then used it as a takeaway to keep on their desk to remind them of lessons learned. I've also used extra items in training programs to help learners apply a new skill. One of my favorites was giving each person a large bag of coated chocolate candies, which they then had to sort by color to create a data set that they'd then use in spreadsheet calculations. It was a unique, hands-on way to learn and apply the topic.

AR objects add value to the learning content in similar ways. You might think of AR like digital props or virtual visual aids. Therefore, facilitators who use AR can take lessons from trainers who have been using visuals and props to enhance the learning experience for years. For example, effective visual aids support the learning objectives and help make a relevant point. The best props are easy and simple to use, without detracting from the learning experience. These reminders are a good starting point from which facilitators can upskill when incorporating AR.

Facilitators can use AR in both traditional classroom and virtual training environments. Each of these use cases provides fodder and will inform our upcoming discussion about facilitation techniques.

Using AR in the Traditional Classroom

Here are a few sample AR activities, starting first with those used in the traditional classroom.

Bring Life to Participant Materials

If a picture is worth a thousand words, then a 3-D, lifelike object must be worth a million. Numerous studies show that using visuals—like images, photos, and diagrams—leads to better learning outcomes (Clark 2020). So, the ability to add AR elements to participant materials (such as handouts, worksheets, and manuals) enhances the learning. Imagine looking at a job aid, pointing your smartphone at a trigger image on it, and seeing an animated version of the instructions appear to walk you through the steps. This 3-D tutorial could walk participants through a complicated procedure, allowing them to explore it on their own before discussing the process with their peers and the expert facilitator.

One of the most difficult issues most facilitators face is having an audience with varying levels of experience. When some participants are novices while others are more advanced, it can be challenging to try to assist both at the same time. AR-embedded participant materials provide a potential solution. The AR objects can provide extra explanations for those who need them. Meanwhile, those who want to move at a faster pace can view bonus AR objects for extra credit. As participants actively engage with the digital content, they become more immersed in the learning experience.

Here's an example. Let's say you work for a large casual restaurant chain and it's time for the new winter menu. The kitchen staff participate in regional roll-out classes to learn about the new dishes and how to prepare them. During the workshop, the facilitator shares a slide with two AR markers on it. Those with less kitchen experience use the one on the right to access a review of the basic knife/cutting skills they'll need to properly prepare the dish. Those with more experience use the marker on the left to watch an animation explaining the recipe's origins and complimentary side dish combinations—information that's helpful and interesting, but not required. Both AR options add value to the participant learning experience, while also helping the workshop facilitator balance everyone's unique needs.

These self-exploration activities transfer control to the learner while still preserving necessary boundaries. In other words, the facilitator invites participants to work on something for a designated amount of time. In a blended learning program, this may be a self-led assignment the participant needs to complete before the next live event. In a classroom context, it may be a 10-, 15-, or 45-minute activity. Either way, the facilitator sets it up but the participants take responsibility for doing the activity and AR enables delivery of information tailored to their needs.

Icebreakers and Opening Activities

Icebreakers and openers capture attention at the start of a workshop. They help participants transition from work to learning and set the tone for the program. Icebreakers usually serve a social purpose by enabling participant introductions, while openers focus more on the content. For example, an icebreaker might ask, "What did you have for breakfast today?" while an opener might ask, "What's your experience with today's topic?" As mentioned previously, openers are almost always the better choice.

One example of an AR-enhanced workshop opener is to place participants in small groups and invite them to scan various images in the room. Each AR object triggers a video with discussion questions or other tasks for the group to complete. As the groups work their way through the maze of activities, they form social bonds, learn about the program, and get motivated to participate. Note that it's important for the facilitator to set up this activity well, so that each group knows exactly what to do and when to do it.

Another workshop opener using AR could be a pop-quiz-style activity that assesses learners' previous experience with the topic. For example, new sales reps could look through the organization's digital product catalog, responding to questions along the way. Each time they scan an AR trigger, they see an either-or poll question alongside the product. This activity entices participant interest in learning the correct responses and assists the facilitator by providing information about the participants' prior knowledge.

Scavenger Hunts

A more advanced type of AR activity allows participants to explore not just around the training room, but around (or even outside) the building. For instance, a hotel chain's new-hire orientation program could go send participants an AR-guided tour of the neighborhood to become better equipped to answer questions from guests about the area. As they follow the route using an AR-enhanced map, location-based AR triggers pop up with relevant information. This is just one of many scavenger-hunt–style activities that could be useful for new hires learning their way around.

Using AR in the Virtual Classroom

Facilitator-led virtual classes are a natural fit for augmented reality applications. First, virtual classroom platforms have several built-in digital features that enhance the online experience. Also, everyone is already using internet-connected devices to access the virtual classroom, which allows for easy access to AR markers. In fact, many virtual class facilitators and participants are already using AR elements without even realizing it! Let's look at a few examples.

Virtual Backgrounds

When I first started teaching virtual facilitators how to show up on camera in an online class, we talked about how to set up your video background. My own backdrop was decorative shelving filled with carefully curated books and awards. What was in the background wasn't as important as simply ensuring it wasn't distracting. But when many people moved to remote work during the COVID-19 pandemic, the ability to create an intentionally designed and curated background was a challenge for many who were working from home in their kitchens and bedrooms. Thus, the advent of virtual backgrounds was a welcome addition to the virtual classroom platform.

The most common virtual background simply blurs the scene, so viewers can see only a fuzzy outline of whatever's behind you. Other backgrounds make it look like you are on vacation or in a perfectly peaceful office setting.

And, as mentioned previously, when we formed teams in one of my recent virtual classes, one group returned from their breakout with matching virtual backgrounds, and then the other groups joined in the fun. It created a sense of community and camaraderie that contributed to engagement and learning.

The biggest evolution of virtual backgrounds, which I find most useful, is the ability to create and use your own images (Figure 6-2). Now, instead of having a blissful tropical scene that looks pretty but isn't practical, facilitators can use AR features to create a background that elevates the learning experience. For example, the facilitator might display a virtual background that includes tech instructions for using the tools, followed by another background that serves as a visual reminder of a key concept.

FIGURE 6-2. Example of a Custom Virtual Background Displayed in Zoom

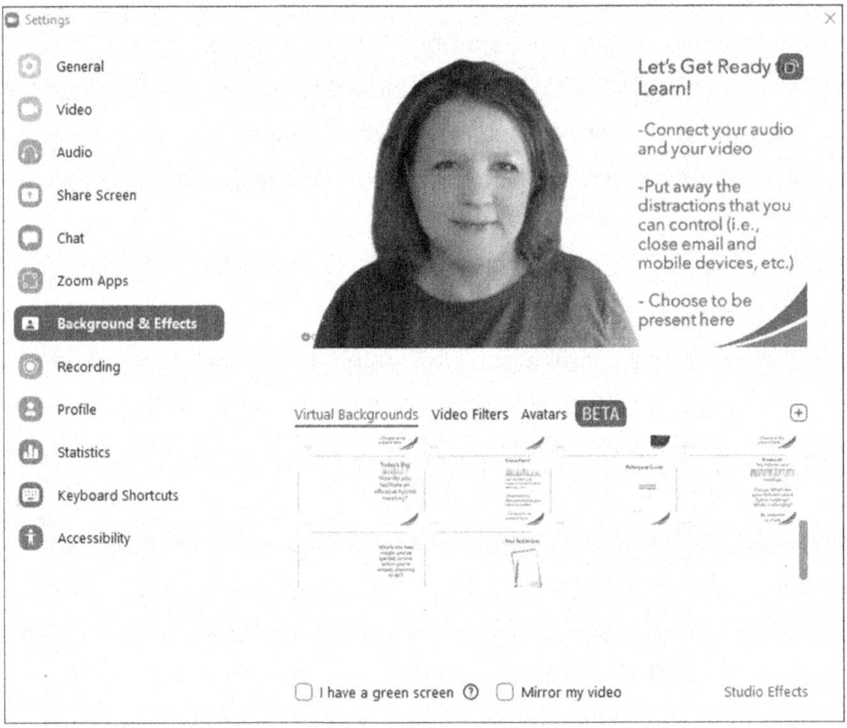

©Zoom Video Communications, Inc. Reprinted with permission.

Facilitators can also use virtual backgrounds to share content in place of sharing slides or screens. I personally use this technique when it's important to use webcams to create a sense of community and foster collaboration. We can stay in gallery view with all participant videos visible, and I can still share content without taking up valuable video space. Virtual backgrounds provide the solution by allowing for shared content without a shared screen. See Figure 6-3 to watch an example of this strategy in action.

FIGURE 6-3. Video Explanation of Using Virtual Backgrounds to Share Content

Filters

At the height of the COVID-19 pandemic, when many meetings were virtual, a video of a lawyer whose virtual platform filter transformed his face into a cat's went viral. His now-famous catchphrase, "I am not a cat!" caused nervous laughter among many who wondered if the same thing could accidentally happen to them.

This unfortunate incident was the result of a built-in video filter, which is another type of augmented reality. It's a digital enhancement of the real world. In the lawyer's case, it wasn't planned, but many facilitators find filters to be a useful feature in virtual classes.

Filters are similar to virtual backgrounds in that they involve webcam video. But they do the opposite—instead of projecting the image behind a person, the digital image is overlaid on top of them. Like other AR objects, the filter seamlessly integrates with the real world. It could completely fill the viewing screen (like a cinematic layered effect) or it could simply enhance one or more components on the screen.

For example, a facilitator could add pop-up messages (think cartoon bubbles) to provide encouraging feedback to participants at appropriate times during a class. Or they could change their overlay scene to indicate a visual transition from one topic to another.

My personal favorite filter is virtual makeup. I use it to smooth out my complexion, and add eyeliner, blush, and lipstick. While that might not seem like a useful facilitation tool, on days when I'm tired or have been on camera most of the day, the makeup serves as a pick-me-up. It helps me look more awake and alive to the participants on the other side of the screen, in turn creating a more positive atmosphere for everyone (Figure 6-4).

FIGURE 6-4. Comparison of Video With and Without Virtual Makeup

Facilitator Overlay on Slides

Part gimmicky, part interesting, and part useful, some virtual classroom platforms now have the ability to integrate the facilitator's webcam video with the slide deck to create one streaming visual aid (Figure 6-5). This combination of reality plus digital image is a quintessential use of AR.

One reason this feature is so useful was noted in a recent study on how the facilitator's eye gaze affected learning retention. The research revealed fascinating insights that showed retention increased when participants followed the facilitator's eyes while looking at onscreen content (Pi et al. 2020). This technique also enhances the learning by integrating conversation and presentation, which makes for a more immersive experience.

FIGURE 6-5. Example of Slides as a Virtual Background in Zoom

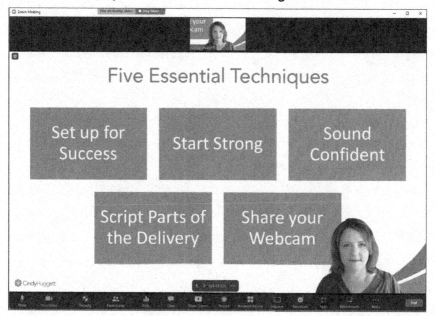

©Zoom Video Communications, Inc. Reprinted with permission.

VOICES FROM THE FIELD

"Audiences demand compelling reasons to pay attention, so when facilitating, I'm constantly using a variety of tools and techniques to keep them engaged while they are learning. The unique feature of integrating video into the slides sparks interest and helps keep them immersed in the learning. Using current technologies is just one way I get massive participant engagement in my virtual classes."
—**Sardék Love, CEO, Sardék Love International**

Hand-Gesture Recognition for Reactions

A relatively new feature in some platforms is hand-gesture recognition. Instead of clicking on the "raise hand" button to indicate agreement, a participant can simply raise their actual hand, which triggers the onscreen digital reaction (Figure 6-6). Or they can clap their hands together to trigger the applause emoji to show up in their video feed.

FIGURE 6-6. Example of Hand Gesture Recognition in Zoom

At first, the novelty of this AR feature makes it fun and attracts attention. But underneath the "wow" factor is a useful technique to increase engagement. The ability to use your hands to indicate emotion and reaction means that you don't have to stop and click, thereby allowing for more natural communication between and among participants. This makes the virtual tools more seamless and integrated. Most important, it helps immerse participants in the learning experience.

Fair warning, though. As a facilitator who talks a lot with my hands, I've needed to adapt my style to stop inadvertent reaction stickers from showing up automatically while I'm speaking. I even turn the feature off and on during different parts of my virtual classes so that I can take advantage of this useful tool, but only when I need it.

Onscreen AR Markers

As mentioned in the restaurant example, adding AR markers into shared slides can add value to a learning experience. When the facilitator seamlessly transitions from a regular slide to one with an AR marker, participants can get involved with the activity. The facilitator explains what to do and sets participants up for success. Because participants in this environment are remote, they may need extra assistance or attention, so the facilitator remains in active listening mode to step in when needed.

AR-embedded activities like these shift the control from the facilitator to the participants because they allow participants to take charge of viewing and interacting with relevant visuals. It also seamlessly integrates digital components into the learning experience.

Self-Directed vs. Facilitator-Led AR Learning Experiences

While it's clear that facilitators can incorporate augmented reality into learning experiences, we should note that there are also many examples of AR-driven self-directed learning. One of personal interest to me is the AR-enabled toothbrush and corresponding app that's helping my young son learn how to properly brush his teeth. The app explains how to set up the toothbrush and get positioned in front of the mobile device camera. It then encourages the user to hunt down and destroy "germ monsters" by brushing all sides of each tooth. The monsters move around my child's mouth in response to the toothbrush, measuring motion and effort. The app's whimsical music and positive feedback make it a fun experience, and the gamification aspect incorporates ratings and rewards for accomplishments. And my son's favorite part is earning child-appropriate AR filters (think funny hats, helmets, glasses, and crowns) that he can use to snap selfies to show off his achievements. This AR experience has him excited to brush his teeth twice a day, and I'm comfortable that he's learning correct brushing techniques.

There are many similar workplace examples too. One of my favorites is from Betty Dannewitz (2020), an immersive experience designer who created a series of AR markers for a small private fitness center. New customers can use these markers to learn how to use the equipment by watching AR-driven demonstrations for procedure, form, and safety. Another example is a product engineer who can use AR markers to quickly access instruction manuals and standard operating procedures whenever they walk onto a factory floor.

So, self-directed AR has its place in learning. A participant needs to learn something, and the AR solution provides the information they need. It's similar to using a web search to find an answer—but with AR, the learning feels more realistic and in context.

Let's summarize the specific skills facilitators need to use AR well in any learning environment.

Five Keys to Successful Facilitation When Using AR in Learning

So far, this chapter has illustrated several key points about successful facilitation using AR. Facilitators need to be comfortable with the technology while keeping it simple for participants. They need to create a safe and trusting environment that makes it OK for participants to explore. They need to adequately prepare in advance—both for themselves and the participants. And they need to remember AR's place in the program, which is to add value beyond the newness and novelty. Here's a summary of these five skills.

1. Prepare in Advance

The facilitator's preparation efforts form the first step of facilitating well with AR. The more prepared a facilitator is to incorporate and use AR in the learning experiences, the more seamless the experience will be for learners.

Preparation includes testing every AR marker in advance to ensure it's working properly. It also means having back-up plans in place just in case something goes wrong. For in-person classes, advance preparation involves making sure the physical room has sufficient wireless internet bandwidth for all participants to connect during AR-driven activities. For virtual classes, it includes setting expectations in advance (such as having their mobile device available for AR viewing) so that the learners all have the necessary equipment required for participation.

2. Comfortable With Technology

Facilitators who are comfortable with technology can seamlessly integrate AR into learning experiences. They won't fumble with their explanations or provide faulty information. Their calm approach to technology-enhanced activity sets the tone for learning.

Let's say there's a trigger from an AR application embedded into the participant materials. A skilled facilitator will quickly explain how to download the app onto a mobile device, assist anyone who needs help in doing so, and then share how to access the AR experience. If participants run into a challenge, the facilitator will be able to respond quickly with an answer, or provide an alternative option.

3. Keep It Simple

The best explanations give the right amount of information—no more, no less—at the right time. Facilitators who master the ability to explain technical instructions in simplistic terms will add value to the learning experience. Participants don't need to know everything; they just need to know enough for learning. When giving instructions for an AR-driven activity, facilitators should make sure participants always know exactly what they are supposed to do, how to do it, and when to do it.

But make sure to avoid taking it to the extreme too—we're working with adult learners, not children. Simple doesn't mean basic or elementary. It means modest and lean.

4. Create a Safe Environment

There's physical safety as well as psychological safety, and skilled facilitators have mastery of both. Some AR experiences can add an element of physical danger if they involve movement. Trip hazards and other potential safety concerns should be addressed and mitigated before anyone begins the activity. Longer AR experiences could cause ergonomic issues by adding to repetitive stress injuries or contributing to poor posture. Facilitators need to be aware and mindful of these potential challenges and take steps to overcome them.

Psychological safety may not initially seem like a concern for an AR learning experience; however, it could pose a potential obstacle to learning. Anytime a facilitator introduces new technology into a learning experience, participants may get frustrated or feel lost. It's essential for the facilitator to be open to questions, no matter how simple they may seem or how many times they have already answered them. Facilitators who establish a supportive environment with positive reinforcement and encouragement will open pathways for learning.

5. Focus on the Learning, Not the Novelty

Everyone knows to focus on learning and on-the-job results, rather than the newness of augmented reality in learning. But it's one thing to say this and another to actually do it. Especially as new technologies emerge, more augmented accessories are developed, and participants become increasingly enamored of the experience. Skilled facilitators will keep their eye on the goal of knowledge transfer and behavior change. They may have fun in the process, but they'll focus on results.

In Summary

Augmented reality is on the cusp of becoming a huge part of our daily routines. It's projected to jump from a $30.7 billion investment in 2021 to an almost $300 billion market by 2024 (Alsop nd). We will see it multiply in our classrooms and other learning experiences, and the time to prepare for it is now.

While AR and VR are often lumped together, they provide very different learning experiences. In the next chapter we will explore the facilitator's role in VR learning.

CHAPTER 7

Facilitating With Virtual Reality

Virtual reality (VR) conjures up a sense of awe and wonder. It's the mystical and futuristic stuff seen in movies. Yet it's also here and now. VR is a part of today's reality, and it's more accessible and available than ever.

Even if you don't have a VR headset, you've likely experienced virtual reality in some way. Maybe you've visited an exceptionally spooky haunted house on Halloween. Or you've seen a 3-D or 4-D movie with amazing special effects. Or you've been to an amusement park and gone on a fully immersive ride. These immersive experiences aren't real, yet they seem real. Therein lies the power of VR: It makes you feel like you are experiencing something when you're not.

That's also the goal of training simulations—to replicate on-the-job situations for the purposes of practice and learning. A training simulation attempts to mimic the job someone will be doing so they can learn how to do it well. The more realistic the practice, the better the learning outcomes (Clark 2020).

Consider the last time you participated in a role-play exercise during a training class. How authentic was it? Was your partner believable in character? Was the environment the same as you would encounter in the workplace? Role play can be a valuable experience, but lots of elements can throw it off, such as shy or reluctant participants, an unrealistic setting, or inadequate props and learning tools. VR offers the opportunity to optimize this type of practice in a learning setting.

Many years ago, I facilitated leadership classes at the headquarters of a large fast-food chain. Its training facility included a full-scale replica of its restaurant, which was used for hands-on exercises in their new manager orientation program. It allowed for real-world practice under authentic conditions. In short, it was awesome. But it also took a lot of resources to run and maintain.

And while that facility worked well for this organization, most training departments don't have the time, money, or resources needed to develop fully realistic simulations for training purposes. The real-life environment may be too detailed, impossible to imitate due to delicate or difficult components, or too dangerous—such as an environment optimized for learning proper responses to safety hazards. In these situations, VR could be part of the answer.

Well-designed training programs have always included hands-on learning activities for practice and application. Flight simulators and other real-world-scenario exercises have been around for a very long time. But today's modern technologies are taking them to unprecedented territory. Virtual reality fuses realistic practice with digital simulations, combining age-old training exercises with modern immersive technology. Josh Bersin (2019), a leading expert in the human resources industry, put it this way: "VR is not a 'technology' being applied to training: it's a new paradigm to learn."

Which leads us to several key questions that need to be answered:

- When are learning experience facilitators needed in VR?
- What role should they play?
- What skills do they need to effectively facilitate in this new environment?

In this chapter, we'll answer these questions while exploring the nuances of using virtual reality in learning experiences.

Using Virtual Reality for Learning

When most people think about VR, it's in the context of gaming. Games are prolific in virtual reality—they are the application it's best known for. While gamification may be a current buzzword in the L&D industry, it doesn't translate to the type of VR learning experiences we're discussing here. In this context, VR is more than entertainment (or "edutainment")—it is focused on achieving learning outcomes and business results.

The most common learning-related VR simulations are used for training-job-related technical skills. For example, an airline pilot can use VR to inspect the aircraft before or after a flight to discover and notate any damage. Or a mechanic can find and fix an electrical problem in a manufacturing facility. Or a new truck driver can learn how to navigate a complex delivery route prior to starting the job. VR allows people to practice complicated skills in a safe digital environment.

The next type of VR learning simulations focus on soft skills like interpersonal relationships, leadership, and communication. For example, public speakers can practice presenting onstage in front of a "live" audience, managers can practice difficult performance conversations, and salespeople can experiment with negotiation techniques for closing a deal. Again, VR provides a digital replica of these environments so that new skills can be learned and practiced in a safe space.

Multiple studies have shown that VR training can drastically reduce seat time, creating massive efficiencies. One report found that skills were learned four times faster via VR training than in classroom-based training (Likens and Eckert 2021). This same study also reported finding a 275 percent increase in learner confidence, resulting in better learning transfer and on-the-job results. The overall positive impact of VR simulations in learning experiences leads to better results.

Example of a VR Learning Experience

To help you visualize a virtual reality learning experience, let's jump into an English-language lesson for business travelers, using a VR platform created by a company named Immerse.

At a designated start time, each remote participant puts on their VR headset and opens the Immerse app. The headset allows them to experience the learning program in a fully immersive environment. To be clear, they aren't together in the same physical room, but they are meeting together in a fully immersive 3-D world designed to help learners unlock fluency. They see one another's avatars in a digital simulation, they hear one another speaking, and they interact with one another and the facilitator (Figure 7-1).

FIGURE 7-1. Participants in Immerse's VR Language Immersion Platform

Reprinted with permission of Immerse.

The facilitator is also remote, but instead of wearing a VR headset, they interact with participants via the Immerse software on their laptop.

During the workshop, participants move from location to location to learn and practice business English in various places: airports, restaurants, boardrooms, and the like. The facilitator establishes the lesson cadence, keeps track of time, selects practice activities, and provides feedback—much like a trainer would do in a traditional classroom. In addition, the facilitator uses the platform to select the VR simulation backdrops, open whiteboards for impromptu collaboration, and interact with the participant avatars.

It's not a long experience—lessons typically last less than an hour. Participants engage throughout the program, completing individual and group tasks, working with partners, interacting with digital objects, and having fun. And most important, they are developing a deeper, more meaningful human connection with one another as a byproduct of learning a new language in virtual reality.

FIGURE 7-2.
Immerse Website With Demo

To see this experience for yourself, aim your smartphone camera at the QR code in Figure 7-2. (No headset needed!)

Types of Learning VR Experiences

The preceding section described just one way VR can be used in a learning program. There are many possible variations. Some VR programs can be purchased off-the-shelf and used as-is to supplement or replace a curriculum. Other VR simulations are custom designed by a developer to serve an organization's specific training purpose.

Regardless of how you procure a VR simulation—build it or buy it—there are four common approaches to incorporating them into a learning experience:

- As an activity in a traditional classroom program
- As an activity in a virtual class
- As a stand-alone virtual event
- As a self-led component in a blended learning journey

Let's review more details about each type.

As an Activity in a Traditional Classroom Program

The best classroom workshops involve participants in hands-on exercises that lead to the learning outcomes. Typical activities may include demonstrations, large group discussions, small group collaboration, and now, VR exercises. When it's time for the VR activity, the facilitator instructs participants to don their assigned headset and enter the digital space. Everyone participates in the learning exercise and, upon completion, they remove their headsets for a debrief discussion.

By bringing VR into the classroom, you can easily visit other locations without leaving the room. Think of it like a staycation field trip! Learners can also get hands-on practice that might not otherwise be feasible.

For example, US-based leadership consulting firm DDI has developed a VR inclusion experience that can be integrated into an organization's leadership training program or other DEI initiatives. The program can be facilitated either in person or as part of a virtual class. During a two-hour traditional classroom experience, participants use VR headsets for an eight-to-10-minute simulation in which they're immersed in a boardroom meeting. After the simulation, a trained facilitator leads everyone in a guided debrief that allows them to reflect on the experience, how it compares to their reality, and the business impact of exclusion and bias. It also prompts them to create a commitment to act upon their lessons learned.

For this type of activity to be successful, the classroom facilitator needs to set the stage appropriately. They need to have the headsets set up and ready for participants to use and clearly explain instructions so everyone knows what to do and when. Facilitators also need to be comfortable enough with the equipment and all aspects of the simulation so the activity runs seamlessly. The training environment may also require preparation; for example, if the simulation requires participants to move or walk around, then define safe spaces with borders for each person. And if challenges arise, the facilitator needs to be prepared to handle them accordingly. We will review these facilitator skills later in the chapter.

As an Activities in a Virtual Class

VR simulations used in a virtual class share many similarities with those used in the traditional classroom. Participants begin by meeting in the virtual platform (see chapter 3 for how to do that well). Then, when the lesson plan calls for it, the facilitator invites participants to start the VR activity. Usually this is initiated by placing a link in chat for everyone to follow. Participants may put on a VR headset for the full 3-D experience or they may instead view the simulation via web browser (although this method isn't ideal). At the end of the activity, participants return to the virtual class to continue the program. It's not unlike leaving a virtual classroom to meet on an external collaboration site (such as an online shared whiteboard), except that the VR activity is fully immersive.

The biggest difference is that the virtual facilitator has much less control over the participant experience. In the traditional classroom, the facilitator provides the equipment and can quickly troubleshoot anything that goes wrong. But because of the nature of the virtual classroom, remote participants have to take responsibility for their own setup. Therefore, the virtual arrangement requires much more advance planning from both the facilitator and participants. For example, how will you distribute the VR equipment to participants—will you ship them all headsets or will they supply their own device? Also, what instructions will you provide so that participant devices are set up with the right software and settings, so that all components are ready to go at the start of the activity. These tasks may sound simple but they are easier said than done!

The first time I used my Google Cardboard headset to participate in a VR activity during a virtual class, I was frustrated by an initial setup instruction that didn't make sense. As simple as the technology seemed, and with as much expertise as I have, I still had trouble figuring out this one step. I persisted and eventually discovered my mistake in time to join the group activity. But this experience reinforced for me the importance of imagining any potential challenges your attendees may encounter and being prepared to mitigate and manage them.

Figure 7-3 on the next page shows an example screenshot of a VR simulation in action during a virtual class.

FIGURE 7-3. Example VR Activity

Printed with permission from eLearning Studios

As a Stand-Alone Virtual Event

In the previous scenario, the VR activity was one element of the virtual class. Participants started in the virtual classroom, moved to the VR experience, and then came back to the classroom. However, it's also possible for the entire live event to fully take place within virtual reality. In other words, instead of moving from 2-D to 3-D, it all happens in 3-D. Participants meet in the virtual room, collaborate in the virtual room, and spend all their time in the virtual room.

These VR meeting spaces are reminiscent of an older online platform called Second Life, which had its heyday in the early 2000s. Participants created avatars and joined virtual spaces to meet and socialize. There were fun activities and games to play, and some organizations even used it for work-related meetings and online events.

Today's VR meeting spaces still use avatars in simulated environments, but technology advancements have changed the parameters and removed some of the stigma around meeting in an immersive virtual room. That's because many of these VR meeting spaces are actually designed for business or hosted by platforms many workplaces are already using. For example, at the time of this writing, you can use Meta's Horizons Workrooms to meet in Zoom VR and Spatial and MootUp power VR meetings in Webex. These online rooms are geared toward collaboration, which is a hallmark of interactive learning experiences.

These fully immersive VR meeting rooms are an emerging technology, and their potential, capabilities, and reach are still evolving. But I think they have a bright future. I predict they are going to explode as more organizations realize the benefit of meeting and learning in the 3-D space. Why commute to an office if you can just don a pair of glasses and be in the office? With VR, you could meet on the factory floor, attend "in-person" meetings, and yes, even actively participate in a training program without leaving the comfort of your home or office. While it might seem unnecessary to join a digital world for everyday work, it allows realistic remote work to occur without physical presence.

The all-encompassing nature of these VR training rooms gives them a big advantage over the standard virtual class: engagement. One of the most common complaints about regular virtual training is that participants often multitask and don't pay attention. Meeting in VR removes that challenge because the participant is immersed—the VR headset blocks out any distractions. It's nearly impossible to multitask when you are engrossed in a VR simulation.

Independent VR Experience

Finally, a participant can use a VR simulation to learn on their own. It could be a completely stand-alone event, or it could be part of a blended learning journey. This type of independent experience may be designed as a solo activity, or it may have built-in social interaction with preprogrammed bots. These bots may be indistinguishable from humans due to their realistic appearance and authentic dialogue.

For example, a new retail salesclerk could join a VR simulation to practice their customer service skills. As they navigate through the digital store, they have to respond to numerous customer questions and assist those who need help. In addition, they'll ring up sales at a cash register, return merchandise to a shelf, and defuse an angry customer who's upset about the return policy. Assuming it's a well-designed simulation, the entire learning experience—including practice and feedback—could go from start to finish without any human intervention at all. The participant could learn a new skill, practice it, and receive feedback on their performance.

This type of independent simulation works best for routine interactions and rote skills. Once a hint of emotion comes into play—for example, if a participant experiences strong feelings as part of the experience—then it's beneficial to have a facilitator help process it. Facilitators can also add value by guiding the experience if there's any element of uncertainty in the simulation. In addition, if the stand-alone event is part of a blended learning journey, a facilitator will likely be involved in some capacity.

But this brings up another question: If a VR experience can use artificial intelligence (AI) to interact with participants, then why would it need a facilitator? Let's explore the answer to that question now.

THE DESIGN FACILITATION CONNECTION

In chapter 1, we established the intimate connection between design and facilitation. This symbiotic relationship holds true for VR simulations as well. Although how to design (rather than facilitate) VR learning experiences is beyond the scope of this book, it's worth mentioning that design quality is of critical importance to learning success. The simulation should be realistic and have fidelity. It should ask participants to complete realistic tasks. And it should be structured appropriately for learning. For more information about designing VR experiences, see the References section.

When Is a Facilitator Needed for VR Learning Experiences?

There's a prevalent assumption that all VR simulations are (or can be) self-contained learning experiences. A person enters the digital space, completes the tasks or experiences in a preprogrammed simulation, and then walks away with lessons learned. If social interaction is needed, it's built into the scenario using artificial intelligence (AI) or other chatbot-style communication.

You have probably interacted with computer-based robots more often than you realize. Their quality improves with every programming iteration and advancement in technology. For example, if you've called a help desk phone number and had to respond to a series of voice prompts before being directed to the right agent, you've interacted with a preprogrammed voice assistant. Or if you've used a text-based chat assistant when seeking customer service on a company's website, then you've communicated with a chatbot. And if you have a smartphone or home digital assistant, you may talk with Siri, Alexa, or Cortana on a regular basis.

Research shows that people are becoming more accustomed to interacting with robots and artificial intelligence than ever before, and some people even prefer communicating with bots over humans (Min et al. 2021; Brown 2019). In fact, many people are unable to tell when they are talking with a digital being instead of a live person. But who among us hasn't argued with Siri or Alexa and gotten frustrated when they misunderstood what you asked? Or been redirected to the wrong place after a mispronunciation?

Now imagine that happening during a learning experience. Maybe you're trying to practice a new skill but the system doesn't recognize your desired action. Or worse, you're in an emotionally charged virtual simulation and the interaction goes off course. Despite a programmer's best intention, if the social interaction with a bot is even slightly off, it will affect the experience and therefore the learning outcomes.

We know from intuition, anecdotal evidence, and research studies that facilitators add value to the learning experience. According to one seminal meta-analysis, "instructional support" provides positive effects on the learning outcomes (Chernikova et al. 2020). Facilitators are—in instructional design terminology—a welcomed "scaffold" to the program.

Other research specifically focused on VR learning also supports this notion. Katie Booth, who spearheaded SAP's Skill Immersion Lab, put it this way: "An effective approach was in the guided discussions instructors at each site facilitated. Our results indicated that this guidance was an influential factor in students learning the content" (Jaehnig 2021).

There are at least four distinct circumstances where facilitators enhance the value of a VR simulation and are needed for its success:

- ▶ **When it's a highly emotional experience.** Participants who become fully immersed in a scenario feel like it's really happening. If the simulation is dangerous (like a safety simulation) or full of conflict (such as a crowd control scenario), then emotions may run high. A skilled facilitator can help the participants process these emotions to both de-escalate their feelings and draw out the lessons learned. If needed, a facilitator can also pause the story line to give participants a quick break from the intensity.

- ▶ **When there's a potential lack of trust.** When participants are wearing a headset during a learning experience, they may be very aware that the simulation is tracking every move, including their eye gaze and hand movements. This realization, even at the subconscious level, may get in the way of learning. Human interaction and guidance can help soften this feeling. Having a trusted facilitator present also helps to increase the level of psychological safety someone feels when wearing the headset.

- ▶ **When human intervention or encouragement is required.** Some VR simulations are designed to be a social experience. For example, a team may work together in the simulation to solve a problem or complete tasks. In these instances, a facilitator may have to change the scenario based upon participant decisions, or encourage the group to persevere and make it to the end.

- ▶ **When participants would benefit from a debrief discussion.** As experienced facilitators already know, learning happens during moments of reflection. By stepping back to analyze their behavior, participants can learn from their reactions to varying situations. Facilitators can help draw out this learning through skilled debrief discussions.

From this point forward, we'll solely focus on VR learning programs that need a facilitator.

The Learning Experience Facilitator's Role in VR

A skilled facilitator can make or break someone's VR learning experience. Do it well, and participants will benefit. Do it poorly or just enough to "make it work," and participants will suffer. Participants may still enjoy a less-than-ideal simulation, but it would only be by happenstance that they walk away with the desired learning outcomes.

Drawing upon the insights provided in the previous chapters, we can surmise that many of the important skills a learning experience facilitator needs for VR are the same as those needed elsewhere. We can also learn from the long history of classroom facilitators who have led simulations or debriefed experiential activities. But a VR learning simulation also requires its own special category of competencies. Its immersive nature, combined with its specialty technology, creates a unique situation that warrants extra attention.

There are three phases of facilitator support for VR:

- ▶ Preparation (before)
- ▶ Facilitation (during)
- ▶ Debriefing (after)

Preparation (Before)

Every type of learning simulation requires advance preparation—setting up the activity, coordinating logistics, getting participants ready, testing the equipment, and more—to ensure success. Getting ready takes time, energy, and effort.

When a simulation runs well, participants likely won't realize the amount of work that went into it. It's like an Olympic athlete who spends countless hours practicing a routine so that it looks easy when they perform it in competition. And that's a good thing. You want a simulation to work smoothly enough that participants experience it as intended, without any mishaps.

Many years ago, I can recall reviewing the facilitator guide to a new leadership program that I would be facilitating the following month. There were pages and pages devoted to just one experiential activity. It listed out every step needed to get ready and then went on to explain how to run the simulation under various circumstances (for example, if there weren't enough participants for every role, if the tables couldn't be moved, or if participants required special accommodations). At the time I thought it was excessive. In hindsight, I was grateful for the advance thought and planning that went into the guidelines, because I ended up using almost every one of those tips at one point or another.

When getting ready to facilitate a VR learning experience, you need to *prepare yourself, prepare the logistics, prepare your equipment,* and *prepare the participants.* The first place to start is with yourself.

VOICES FROM THE FIELD

"I've been a professional facilitator for more than 10 years and, due to a client request, I needed to quickly learn how to facilitate in a VR environment. To start, I spent about an hour in VR every day, three to four nights per week. I tried out different apps, different games, and different experiences. I learned how to orient myself and the different ways you can move around. While VR is intuitive, it's still important not to underestimate how much time it takes to get comfortable."
—Scott Cooksey, Owner, Leadout Performance Group

Prepare Yourself: Get Familiar With the Equipment and the Simulation

If you are new to VR, start by getting comfortable with the equipment. Wear the headset, use the controllers, and get used to how everything works. You want to be fully prepared to show someone else how to use the tools.

Next, if you haven't already, go through the simulation as a participant. If there are multiple roles or multiple scenes, explore each one. Make sure you know what everything looks like and how it feels when you're in the midst of it. If the simulation has a fully immersive version and a desktop VR version, do each one. Get thoroughly familiar with the content, the technology, and every other component of the program.

Part of the reason for this preparation step is you want to become a subject matter expert in the simulation. When you know it well, you can facilitate it well.

In addition, if you know how the simulation is supposed to work, you'll more easily recognize when something goes wrong. You won't waste mental energy in the moment trying to figure things out; instead, you can redirect those thoughts to helping participants. For example, if a participant picks up a digital object in the virtual room and it doesn't do what they expect, you will already be prepared to address it, instead of wondering whether to step in to help. Or if a participant struggles to complete a task, you'll recognize if that struggle is caused by their lack of knowledge or something broken in the activity. The more you know about the simulation, the easier it will be to guide participants through it.

VOICES FROM THE FIELD

"Facilitators must get comfortable in the VR headset themselves and confident demonstrating the headset to others. As I was preparing to facilitate, I practiced explaining the tech to as many people as I could, so that I could effortlessly guide my participants." —**Angelle Lafrance, Director, Learning Systems, DDI**

Prepare the Logistics

Whether your VR event takes place remotely or in the classroom, there's an essential need for well-planned logistics. It takes time and a hyper-focus on details to ensure all goes well.

For instance, if you, the facilitator, are responsible for setting up the classroom, you'll need to arrange the tables and chairs and other participant materials, as well as set up the VR headsets. You'll need to ensure the headsets are all fully charged, are able to connect to the internet, have the most current software, and are easily accessible. If the headsets are wired, you'll need to organize the cables and take time to tape them down or otherwise secure them to avoid fall hazards. In addition, you may need to set up peripheral accessories such as earphones and handheld controllers. Again, these items need to be charged and ready to go before the start time. See Figure 7-4 for an example of how one facilitator arranged his classroom equipment.

FIGURE 7-4. VR Headsets Ready for Use in the Classroom

Printed with permission from Bill Treasurer, CEO, GiantLeap Consulting

If you're concerned about connecting multiple devices to the internet at the same time, then testing out the wireless bandwidth connectivity will be an important step. You don't want the VR simulation to freeze or be choppy, otherwise it won't be realistic, and the learning point could be lost.

If movement is part of the experience, you may need to create designated boundary lines for each headset to ensure that participants stay inside their assigned play space. This step could potentially require you to put on each headset and go through the motions one by one to create each individual space.

If you're fortunate enough to have a dedicated training room, then the headsets and other equipment may just "live" there in an assigned storage space. But if you're moving from location to location, you'll need to plan ahead and determine how to transport the headsets to the classroom. Will you hand carry them? Ship them? Something else? You'll also need to determine how early to arrive for setup. Is an hour long enough, or do you need to schedule additional time the day before? These minor details all add up to major impact on your simulation's success.

VOICES FROM THE FIELD

In Giant Leap Consulting's virtual reality experience, we put participants' courageous leadership and teamwork to the test. Our fully immersive team training simulation is designed to help participants "catch themselves being themselves" in a psychologically safe environment. The result is better team cohesion and improved leadership behaviors.

For the classroom version of this experience, we've learned the importance of advance setup. Taking the time to check and prep the headsets ensures a positive learning experience for everyone. We have reliable processes in place for a seamless start and a team of expert facilitators ready to deliver.

—**Bill Treasurer, CEO, Giant Leap Consulting**

As a traveling trainer, I used to carry everything I needed for my workshops on airplanes. I even had a special padded suitcase designed to protect the sensitive devices. More recently, I used a cargo service to ship my equipment in advance. Each method required intentional thought. If I brought everything with me, I'd need to be able to access the classroom early enough for setup. If I shipped them, I'd need to schedule when the supplies would arrive and make arrangements for how they would get to the classroom. I can't tell you how many times I arrived hours before a workshop or even the day before and, despite having a confirmed arrival signature, not be able to find the shipment because it was lost somewhere in the building.

While these initial tasks may seem unimportant or frivolous, they are critical for a successful setup. And ultimately, they are the facilitator's responsibility. Even with a support team in place, you are the one who has to stand in front of participants. The facilitator's primary job is to enable learning; so, if the program outcomes depend upon the simulation, you need to make sure it works.

Prepare Your Own Equipment

If the simulation calls for an active facilitator role, then you'll also need to set up your own equipment. In other words, if you're going to join participants in the digital environment as an avatar, then you need to make sure your software is ready to go. As a side note, make sure that your avatar is appropriate for the audience and the simulation. For example, if you're working with medical professionals, you can dress your avatar in scrubs. But if you're working with frontline retail workers, you may want your avatar to be dressed in the company uniform.

If participants are going to hear your voice during the activity, spend time testing your audio for clarity. Use a headset instead of relying on the device's microphone. And make sure your internet bandwidth is strong enough to support the audio stream. If the sound is OK but not great, a participant might not be able to articulate why the simulation seems off; they just know subconsciously that it is. Research has shown that lower audio quality decreases the participant experience (Oh, Bailenson, and Welch 2018). Since VR simulations surround participants with 360 degree audio, your sound quality is especially important.

OTHER ROLES NEEDED

It's been said that it takes a village to raise a child—it may also take a village to create a seamless VR learning experience. For example, the designer and developer create an authentic simulation and an operations coordinator helps manage the overall program logistics. You likely also need tech support for the equipment and to help participants with setup. And someone to clean and sanitize any shared devices between use.

I recommend having at least one tech support person available during the facilitated VR activity. While a facilitator could take time to help a participant get into the simulation, doing so will draw their attention away from the other participants who have already successfully connected. Instead, the tech support person can step in to assist participants while the facilitator focuses on running the simulation. This helps to create a better overall experience. This tech assistant role is parallel to the producer's role in the virtual classroom.

Additionally, even if a VR program is designed with accessibility in mind, you may still encounter learners with accessibility issues on the day of. You and your tech support should both be fully aware of and knowledgeable about any accommodations that have been made to the training for their needs.

So yes, it's possible for the facilitator to be a one-person show and handle all the responsibilities. However, if the resources are available, it's best to involve multiple people.

Prepare Participants

As a facilitator, one of your key responsibilities under any circumstance is to create a safe, comfortable, trusting environment for participants—to remove obstacles that would otherwise get in the way of learning. It's important for this to happen in the classroom, but it doesn't start there. It begins in advance of the learning event.

Some people refer to the participant preparation step as pre-work. However, that's my least favorite description to use, mostly because it's a weak term with a tarnished perception. It's often overlooked and undervalued. Participants usually don't complete the pre-work, which then creates a conundrum for everyone.

So, to successfully prepare participants prior to a VR learning experience, emphasize the importance of action in all advance communication. Your aim is to get them ready. You may not have control over whether they complete their part of the tasks, but you will have done everything you can to help. The saying "You can lead a horse to water, but you can't make them drink" may seem to apply to this conversation. But I'm telling you to go one step further and add sugar to the water. Take on the responsibility of doing as much as possible to prepare participants in advance of the event.

So what exactly should you do? First and foremost, if participants are going to be using VR headsets in their own locations, you need to confirm that they have all received their headset from you or that their personal headset is compatible. If they're setting up their own headset, you need to communicate the tech specs needed—everything from bandwidth requirements to software downloads. You'll also need to check in with them to confirm it's all set and ready to go.

If the participants are new to VR, you may also need to teach them how to walk through the initial equipment setup. For example, you might need to explain how to measure their IPD (interpupillary distance) to adjust the headset for proper fit and clear vision. If they wear glasses, you may need to show them how to install an insert. You may also need to help them install the simulation software and establish location markers for boundaries. Over time, as more and more people gain experience using the VR equipment, this setup assistance will become less necessary. Today it's a useful addition for most.

For efficiency and convenience, you may ask IT partners or others in the organization to help participants with their equipment setup. Or, you could create a video for participants to watch, hold an orientation session, or provide detailed job aids. However it's done, and whatever your role in the process, it's still ultimately your responsibility to ensure it happens. At minimum, facilitators should verify that participants have what they need to engage in the simulation. In addition, if participants have disclosed their accessibility needs in advance, you can research potential solutions and help them learn how to use the technology in a way that is adapted to them.

Proper participant preparation also involves ensuring more than physical and technology comfort. It's important to create a learning environment with emotional security and support. You don't want participants to be too stressed out to learn.

One potential area for concern is fear of the unknown. If it's someone's first time in a VR simulation, they may approach it with trepidation. For example, they may have heard that VR can cause motion sickness and be worried about that. Or maybe they're anxious about interacting with others. You can help reduce participant anxiety by letting them know in advance exactly what to expect. For example, tell them what they'll see onscreen upon joining, and what the first two or three actions will be. You may need to keep some aspects of the simulation hidden if discovery is part of the program, but in general, the more you tell them, the more comfortable they will feel.

Also, be available to answer their questions. The last thing you want is for frustration with the technology, concern over confidentiality, or some other minor issue to get in their way of learning. Facilitators who are absorbed in their own preparation may miss seeing these participant needs, and while they may seem like small things, they can have a big impact on the learning.

Facilitating in the Moment (During)

Facilitators who actively partake in a VR simulation should remember their primary role: to successfully enable learning. They need to be expert coaches, active listeners, and able to draw out learning points. They also need to be flexible, quick to respond, comfortable with the technology, and able to seamlessly guide participants though the program. Effective VR facilitators have a special set of skills.

For example, during an in-person VR simulation exercise, skilled facilitators know to tread gently around participants in headsets. They avoid startling anyone already in their headset because the person may not realize the facilitator is standing next to them. Instead, they will carefully tap a participant on the shoulder or speak loud enough for them to hear someone approaching.

There are two types of VR facilitators: those who watch the simulation unfold from an external viewpoint and those who play an actual role in the simulation. The external observer facilitator—*the simulation sage*—watches behaviors, tracks performance, and manipulates the environment. In other contexts, specifically the gaming world, this role is called a "puppet master" and their job is to manipulate the environment to force outcomes. The learning experience facilitator, on the other hand, is running the simulation to create a learning outcome, not entertainment. We want participants to succeed and learn. Facilitators may change the settings, switch scenes, or cause situations to happen, but it is always with the learners' best interest in mind.

TWO TYPES OF VR FACILITATORS
- **Simulation Sage:** External observer, possibly with simulation controls
- **Active Agent:** Immersed alongside the participants

A VR facilitator who plays an actual role in the simulation is an ***active agent.*** This type of facilitator is immersed in the digital environment alongside participants, interacting and communicating as part of the scene. For example, they could be acting as the participants' practice partner or demonstrating how to complete tasks so that learners can practice on their own. Active agents may be a tour guide or subject matter expert, leading participants through the digital world. Either way, this second type of facilitator is an active contributor inside of the virtual experience.

Both types of facilitators—the *simulation sage* and the *active agent*—have to begin the VR learning experience by setting clear guidelines and expectations. Participants need to know what to do when they enter the virtual world, what guidelines to follow, and how to interact with others. For example, you might provide a quick overview of commands and controls. Or you might provide instructions for the participants to explore the room while everyone is joining in. Make sure your verbal and visual directions are short, simple, and extra clear. However, keep in mind that it can be difficult to read text while wearing VR lenses.

In a group setting, the facilitator should establish ground rules for behavior. At minimum these guidelines need to address respect and inclusion, letting everyone know what's acceptable behavior. Because this is new territory for many people, they might not realize that moving an object that someone else just moved could be interpreted as aggressive behavior. Or they might not recognize that talking over someone, or invading another avatar's personal digital space, can be perceived as rude and offensive.

In addition, keep in mind that participants who don't trust other participants will have a harder time getting into the simulation and focusing on the learning experience. This is why it's so important to establish high levels of trust and create a safe learning environment for all.

**SAMPLE GROUND RULES
FOR A COLLABORATIVE VR SIMULATION:**
- Avoid moving into another participants' personal space in the digital environment. Maintain appropriate distance.
- Don't grab an object out of someone's hand or near someone's space. They may be trying to manipulate it. Wait for your turn.
- Be aware of your audio volume and background noise. Use "mute" just like you would in a videoconference.

Special Considerations for the Simulation Sage

As a simulation sage facilitator who stays outside the learning environment but has direct control over it, there are a few important guidelines to keep in mind.

First, if you're going to press a button and change the scene, tell people before you do it! Remember that when participants are fully immersed in the scenario it can be quite jarring if they're standing in one location and then all of a sudden moved to a new location without warning. The same rule applies when changing avatars during a scenario or even between scenes. If a simulation character's long, dark hair and fancy dress suddenly change to short, red hair and a military uniform, that quick change likely needs explanation. These changes could be too overwhelming in the moment and decrease the effectiveness of the learning experience.

A second essential consideration in a simulation is deciding when to step in versus when to let participants go. For instance, do you interfere and make a change if you're watching a scene unfold and participants make a decision that will alter the final outcome?

While circumstances may occasionally require intervention, facilitator interference should be minimal. It's not about the facilitator or the facilitator's expertise; it's about the learner. Whether a simulation is successful is often not determined by the actual activity, but what someone learns from it. The choices they make and the reflections on why they made those decisions is where the learning occurs. How a participant reacted in the moment can be ripe for review and reflection. Nowhere is this more clear than in a virtual reality simulation.

I used to facilitate an experiential business simulation that taught managers how their everyday decisions affected the organization's bottom line. Participants were faced with a series of choices and, based upon their reactions, entered prescribed data into a fictional accounting system. At the end of each pretend quarter, we examined the performance of each group's balance sheet, just like an executive team would do. The teams reflected on their decisions, and used that information to make a new set of choices each round. At the very end of the simulation, we led the group through a detailed reflection and debrief to draw out many key learning points. One of my colleagues always wanted to share an optimal end-of-year answer—what they could have done throughout the simulation to achieve the best financial results. However, I always resisted sharing this information, because in the context of learning, the final answer didn't matter. Instead, the knowledge gain was in the process, taking place throughout the activity.

In a similar vein, participants in a VR simulation rarely need to achieve one right answer or outcome to learn. Facilitators should avoid interrupting the learners' choices and let the scenario play out. It's OK if it's not perfect; it can still be a learning experience. Let them suffer safe consequences. Interruptions will break the learning flow and affect immersion.

Special Considerations for the Active Agent

In addition to playing your part in the simulation, the active agent facilitator requires extra skill in two key areas: improvisation and authentic voice.

Acting and Improv Skills

Improvisational skills have long been heralded as an effective technique for classroom facilitators. There are numerous books, articles, and even workshops devoted to bringing improv methods into the learning experience for better results (McKnight and Scruggs 2008). For example, the "Yes, and" technique encourages new ideas to surface during conversations. And storytelling helps learners connect to content and remember it beyond the experience (Yorton 2013).

One well-known VR training provider, Mursion, includes professional acting experience as a qualification when hiring for their facilitator roles (called sim specialists). The company believes that acting skills give facilitators "the flexibility and dexterity to inhabit several characters and think fast on their feet" (mursion.devops 2020).

Using an Authentic and Effective Voice

Several factors point to the importance of facilitator authenticity in a VR simulation, as well as its impact on the learning environment. First, a speaker's voice in any multimedia learning experience will influence the outcomes. What a facilitator says should be conversational (as opposed to reading from a script) and feel natural (Mayer 2014). In other types of online learning, it's been demonstrated that participants learn better when they hear a polite, friendly human voice (Clark and Mayer 2013). This emphasizes the significance of the facilitator's preprogram preparation. They need to be familiar enough with the simulation story line to play along, without sounding contrived or too scripted.

In addition, as mentioned earlier, the facilitator's audio quality itself may affect the learning outcomes (Oh, Bailenson, and Welch 2018). When speaking to participants in a VR simulation, facilitators need to be clearly heard and understood. Therefore, active agent facilitators should pay extra attention to their audio connections and ensure they have sufficient bandwidth, noise-canceling headsets, and a clear voice.

At the end of this chapter, you'll find a VR Facilitation Troubleshooting Guide, which will help you with common situations that may arise, along with suggestions on how to best respond to them.

Debrief (After)

When most people think about a hands-on experiential learning activity, they think of the facilitator's actions after the exercise. The same is true in a VR simulation. The facilitator's ability to provide effective feedback and lead meaningful debrief discussions plays a key role in learning transfer. This facilitator skill is where the proverbial rubber meets the road.

Upon conclusion of a VR learning simulation—and regardless of the facilitator's role during it (simulation sage, active agent, or nothing at all)—this is the time to provide feedback and examine what happened. There may also be logistical considerations to address, such as clean-up and reporting.

Provide Feedback

Providing feedback is a key facilitator responsibility in any learning environment. In an immersive VR experience, some feedback may be provided in real time during the simulation, while other feedback may occur later. If the experience was recorded like a movie (called "machinima"), it could be used later for reflection and debrief. This is similar to a sports team watching game film to determine strengths and weaknesses, with the goal of improving for next time.

Whenever feedback is provided in a group setting, my preferred method is to start by asking a participant, "What went well from your perspective?" and then listening carefully to their answer. If I agree with the assessment, I'll validate it with my own concrete observations. If their observations were incorrect for any reason, I'll share my viewpoint backed by a detailed explanation. I make sure my feedback is always positive, emphasizing what they did well without sugarcoating any changes that need to be made.

VR facilitators must master the art of giving effective feedback. One common method used by many expert facilitators across all learning environments is the Center for Creative Leadership's SBI model (Leading Effectively Staff 2020). In it, a facilitator shares three specific things when providing feedback: the situation, the observed behavior, and the impact of that behavior. This approach is an effective way to give feedback in all scenarios, including VR.

Debrief Discussion

Another classic facilitator responsibility is to debrief learning activities. While debriefing a VR simulation uses the same techniques as any other type of simulation, VR facilitators also need to account for the digital saturation of the experience. Because the VR learning experience is so realistic, participants are more likely to feel higher levels of emotion than in a typical training scenario. Thus, they may need more time to reflect individually or in small groups before discussing what happened. Participants may also need to talk more or longer due to the rich simulation that just occurred.

There are many different debriefing models; my favorite is Driscoll's "What? So what? Now what?" technique (Driscoll and Teh 2001). With this method you ask participants to verbalize what they experienced. Then you ask about the importance of the experience and how it relates to their current realities. For instance, "How was that experience similar to your workplace environment?" falls in the "So what?" category. Finally, the line of questioning moves to "Now what?" which probes the learner's ability to apply their new discoveries.

In addition to this line of debrief questioning, it's also a good idea to ask participants about their feelings and thoughts during the experience. By asking them to name emotions in addition to their actions, they may uncover additional insight.

Post-Event Logistics

Just like a classroom trainer turns off the projector, erases the whiteboard, and rearranges the furniture back to its original position, a VR facilitator has post-event tasks to complete. A simulation may need to be rewound to its starting point, or a VR room reset to the original setup. Facilitators may also be responsible for cleaning, sanitizing, and powering down the headsets. The equipment may need to be shipped back home or to the next location. In addition, facilitators should make sure to file any necessary reports, reflect on the experience for their own lessons learned, and get ready for the next time.

CASE STUDY Facilitators and VR at Farmers Insurance

VR training has helped shorten the experience curve for claims adjusters at Farmers Insurance®. And a big part of that is due to the involvement of facilitators. The value they add to the VR program is key, says Jessica DeCanio, head of claims training at Farmers®. "The facilitator helps ensure that learning is taking place and that somebody isn't just walking through it like a video game," she says.

Claims adjusters investigate cases such as property damage caused by water or fire, or auto damage and injuries. They make an assessment for claims with customers and businesses. Farmers traditional training method includes sending adjusters to in situ training at a house set up with different scenarios that they role-play to learn the business. The decision to include VR in the training mix accelerated that learning process. It also allowed Farmers to be ahead of the curve in adapting to a virtual setting during the COVID-19 pandemic.

Rather than being limited to the scenarios created in their real-life training house, employees can use VR to work through an expansive range of damage assessments and more quickly gain additional knowledge and skill.

But it's the facilitator's input that helps turn the experience into learning. As the trainee progresses through the VR scenarios, the facilitator is able to observe and provide relevant coaching. "The facilitator will ask, 'Why did you make that choice? What would have happened if you'd done this instead? Let's step back and look at it a different way.' They are there to make sure that learning is occurring," she explains.

Facilitators also enable Farmers to offer this training as a group experience. "Right now, we have 30 VR headsets spread among our large locations. But if one person has the headset on, we can broadcast what they're going through on a big screen, and the entire class can be engaged in capturing that experience," Jessica says. The facilitator will enable group conversations by asking questions such as, "What do you think the operator should do next?" and coaching everyone through the experience to create a sense of community learning. In addition, Farmers VR courses have the ability to be used either via headset or desktop, enabling greater access.

Because VR is still relatively new, facilitators can benefit from upskilling and extra support. For Jessica, that has meant creating facilitator guides that cover both the technical side (how to troubleshoot if a trainee is struggling to use the equipment or there's a glitch) and the learning side.

"It's a 50–50 mix of developing a 'help desk' mentality and addressing the objectives of the training—what are we hoping the trainees get out of the experience and how, as a facilitator, do you get the most out of this scenario. How do you coach them through, either one-on-one or in a group?"

Jessica says they also run train-the-trainer sessions in which facilitators can experience using VR themselves. Much of that is directed at helping facilitators manage the change to VR and, she says, "feel like they're part of this."

As Jessica points out, VR is just one more modality for learning professionals to have in their toolkit and it's worth exploring. "Curiosity is the thing I would encourage most for facilitators," she says. "So when the right learning challenge comes in front of them, they know enough to be able to confidently recommend using VR. That could make a difference from a facilitator perspective—being ready for it."

In Summary

This chapter contained a lot of information for VR facilitators. And while it's easy to understand how overwhelming it can feel to consider the move from a classroom to a virtual simulation, many of the fundamental facilitator skills still apply in this new environment. Rest assured in your current skill set, and take steps toward expanding it, one program at a time.

How do you know if you're ready to facilitate in VR? And how do you get started? Just do it. Take time to practice, experiment, and learn. In the next chapter, we'll look at ways you can continue to hone your skills as a facilitator, and to ensure you're always learning.

VR Facilitation Troubleshooting Guide

Situation	Suggested Response
Participant experiences motion sickness	This happens when there's a sensory disconnect, which causes the body to feel something different from what the eyes are seeing. To overcome this challenge, have the person: ▶ Use teleporting instead of "walking" to switch between scenes ▶ Place a fan in front of them so they can feel cool air flowing ▶ Make sure the headset fits properly ▶ Take off the headset, take a short break ▶ Sit down (if they're currently standing) and look off into the distance

Situation	Suggested Response
The scenario becomes too intense	A participant may become overwhelmed with unwanted sensations during a digital simulation. Or they may have an unexpected emotional reaction that interferes with their ability to learn. If this happens, invite them to remove their headset and take a short break. (They often forget that they can do this!) Help them process through the emotions using the debriefing techniques found in the next section. Allowing for opt-outs is another option—ask participants if they want to continue or move on.
Unexpected tech issues occur	As is the case with all technology-enabled learning programs, sometimes tech challenges get in the way. In VR simulations, it could be a headset running out of battery power, or a glitch in the story line. When something unexpected happens, determine if it's affecting only one participant, or if it's a global issue affecting everyone. Make a quick determination if the VR simulation should be stopped, or if it can continue despite the issue. It's a good idea to assign a dedicated tech support person to manage these issues.
Some participants wear a VR headset but others are using PC VR	If it's a group collaboration activity, then assign roles accordingly. Use job aids or other performance support techniques to ensure everyone knows where to click or how to use the commands. As part of preparation, the facilitator should get familiar with both instances of the simulation so that they can speak to either environment.
A participant becomes disruptive	Establish ground rules in advance to proactively prevent disruptions. If they occur anyway, consider the root cause. If the participant is unknowingly disruptive (such as an odd echo coming from their audio connection), work with them to troubleshoot and eliminate the distraction. If they are deliberately choosing to display poor behavior, remove them from the scenario, focus on the remaining learners, and address the disruptive participant privately afterward.

CHAPTER 8
The Facilitator of the Future

There's no question that the facilitator role is changing. The bigger question is what you can do to prepare yourself to stay relevant as a training professional. Change is constant in this industry, and if you're not growing in your role, you will become stagnant and eventually irrelevant. By staying current and keeping your eyes on the horizon of what's next, you will continue to grow and learn, and you will continue adding value to modern learning experiences. This is how you become the learning experience facilitator of the future.

An iconic ride at Walt Disney World in Florida is Walt Disney's Carousel of Progress, which was originally built for the 1964 New York World's Fair. During the rotating ride you "follow an American family over four generations of progress and watch technology transform their lives" (WDW nd). Each scene—which transitions from the early 1900s to the early 2000s—presents a snapshot in time of the family's lifestyle. The story line highlights innovations in technology, such as air-conditioning, washing machines, and cooking appliances. When the ride was updated in 1993, the final scene was redesigned to showcase an imagined Christmas in the 2000s, complete with mentions of voice-activated technology, laser discs, and VR headsets. As a modern rider, when you look at the scene, you know they did their best but didn't quite hit the mark. It was close, but just enough to be obviously wrong.

That's the challenge of trying to predict the future of anything. We can make informed guesses, but no one really knows what will happen. For example, a good weather forecast can accurately predict only the immediate future. Experts try to share long-term forecasts (10–14 days), but accuracy improves with closeness. Truly long-range forecasts—such as those relied upon by farmers and transportation engineers (or found in the annual

Farmers' Almanac)—are based upon historical trend data and scientific estimations. There's value in making predictions and educated guesses; yet, as the saying goes, hindsight is always 20/20.

On that note, this chapter is full of my best predictions about the facilitator role of the future. In the near-term, these trends are almost certain to be here before we know it. In the longer term, they're my estimates for what to expect. In addition, I'll share strategies facilitators can use to keep up with the industry and grow their skills.

The Evolving Facilitator Role

Throughout my more than 30-year career in workplace learning, I've heard people say many times and in many different contexts that the facilitator role will soon be obsolete. Sometimes it's in reference to the death of the traditional classroom. Other times it's the downfall of all formal training initiatives in favor of informal learning. Still other comments have been made surrounding the rise of self-directed learning, or in the depth and breadth of information available freely online.

As this book has already established, a skilled facilitator can play an active part in all types of learning. Let's first look at where the facilitator role may be going, followed by three categories of strategies you can follow to evolve along with it.

What elements will characterize the facilitator of the future? I predict future facilitators will experience *boundaryless training, ubiquitous technology,* and *specialized tailoring.* Let's explore each of these further.

Boundaryless Training

Our current boundaries of time and place are artificially created. From ancient sundials to the wristwatch, we "invented" seconds, minutes, and hours to help us calculate this thing we call time. Aside from sunup to sundown, every other measure of time was created and then agreed upon by society.

For example, think about why it's common for professionals to work from 8 a.m. to 5 p.m. local time. Or why we typically schedule 60-minute meetings. The eight-hour workday became standard in the era of manufacturing schedules to make sense in settings with shift work. And meetings default to 60 minutes on most electronic calendars. In other words, their foundation is based on agreed upon but artificially imposed standards. And because they aren't real boundaries, these agreements can change. We can break free from the idea that work and learning have to be done during certain hours of the day. And we can change the idea that classes have to be taught on a Tuesday morning (or whatever standard time your organization uses).

About 25 years ago, my direct supervisor was an older gentleman who wanted to ensure his management team was working a "standard" workday. He measured this by checking to see who was logged in to our organization's instant messenger system. I recall thinking at the time, *Just because my computer is connected doesn't mean that my mind is working*. By 8 a.m. I may have already dealt with a facilitator staffing problem, made arrangements to meet a client later in the day, and worked on quarterly plans. Or, I may have not yet done anything because of a late-night project the previous day. His method was, and still is, based on an artificial test governed by boundary-based thinking.

Global time zones are another fabricated boundary. It's obviously day and night at different times in different parts of the world. That natural rhythm is set. And the standardization of communicated times help us as a society to get work done. Yet time zones don't need to dictate working hours. For example, it's easy to have meetings with attendees across time zones using the tools and technology available to us today.

Yes, there are circumstances where boundaries still make sense—such as labor laws that prevent someone from working off the clock or overtime rules that keep an employee from participating in a time-based learning activity. Additionally, learners will still want their sleep schedules respected, and expect to have time for their families and nonwork life.

Yet these situations don't negate the overall trend toward releasing time-constrained boundaries.

Likewise, geographic boundaries have been established on maps and therefore in our minds. Not just country separators but also cities, counties, states, and regions. These margins make sense in the physical world. For example, in the past, a facilitator might have said, "I'm the regional sales trainer for the Southeast. I work from 9 a.m. to 5 p.m. and teach classes for my local employees starting at 10 a.m. on Tuesdays, Wednesdays, and Thursdays." However, this doesn't always translate to the online world.

The learning experience facilitator of the future isn't defined by these boundaries. It's not unusual for a facilitator to log in to a course platform at 6 a.m. local time (before they've even had their morning coffee) or teach a 9 p.m. class with participants located halfway around the world. Attendees from various "regions" can connect in a learning cohort and use technology tools to break down language barriers. Instead of clocking into a standard workday and teaching a certain number of classes, a facilitator's value can be measured in other ways. It's a new way of thinking about hours worked—measuring output and results instead of the number of hours on a clock.

One more note about boundaries—some global organizations have already adopted this style of working. They have set aside time-based restrictions in favor of output and results and truly embrace having a diverse workforce by allowing for round-the-clock learning opportunities. But for many organizations and training departments, the idea of breaking boundaries is a revolutionary concept. There's tension over remote-working policies and flexible working arrangements, which affects learning strategies. It's clear that many organizations still have a long way to go in truly adopting training programs that transcend time and geographical boundaries.

Ubiquitous Technology

I spent a lot of time walking across an extremely hilly campus to get to the computer lab when I was in college. So, it was a big deal for my roommates and me to get a desktop computer in our apartment. (We traded a year of housekeeping services for our landlord to get it for us. As much as we enjoyed having the desktop, in hindsight we probably should have kept the housekeeping services.) Each time we needed to connect the computer to the university's systems, we had to wait several minutes for the dial-up modem to connect. And we went through a lot of floppy discs to save and transfer files.

Compare that experience with today's college students, who have full computer power and an always-connected internet device that fits in the palm of their hand. Most business professionals do as well. According to Pew Internet Research, more than 5 billion people have a mobile device and more than half of those are smartphones (Silver 2019).

Sadly, I recognize that this may not be your experience. A digital divide still exists in many areas of the world, including within the US. Many people still lack high-quality internet or the resources to purchase connected devices. Fortunately, the gap is narrowing due to technology and other innovations, including the addition of 5G networks, satellite internet, and affordable tablet devices. We are moving toward an always-connected society.

In a similar vein, right now, at least in the US, many professionals wear some type of smart watch. I predict that it won't be long before smart glasses (and/or smart contacts) become the norm. They'll be stylish, blue-light-blocking, internet-connected devices that respond to eye movement and verbal commands. This combination of biometrics and wearables, along with increasingly accessible internet access, will no longer live just in movies but in our everyday lives.

With always-connected learners comes always-accessible facilitators. As discussed in chapter 5, the facilitator's role of guiding participants through a sequence of learning events has exploded in popularity and acceptance. And when facilitators and participants adopt more wearables, we'll see increased expectations for timely communications.

I'm reminded of the time my first and only son was born. It was an extremely full season of intertwined work and life. I had just written my second book on virtual training and remember proofreading it while nursing my newborn. I felt tired and drained and energized all at the same time. I wondered how I would be able to manage the next few months and years of balancing a child with building a business. After confiding in a wise and trusted friend about my fears, she reminded me that this baby joined our family for a reason and advised me to "bring him along with you; he will adapt." I'll never forget those early years of trying to plan client meetings and virtual classes around a toddler's nap schedules. While some professionals can fully separate work and home, I found that her sage words helped—what worked best for me was to integrate the two. So it wasn't unusual for me to respond to emails from my smartphone after rocking him to sleep, or to plan a full day at the park knowing that I'd take a client call while watching him play.

I believe that this type of ubiquitous technology integration will happen for facilitators of the future as well. We'll be juggling tasks and projects along with communicating and coaching—giving our full attention to the present moment without sacrificing quality.

Learning experience facilitators will be always connected. Checking in with a learning cohort will become seamless, making it easier to communicate and build relationships. Communications between facilitators and among learners will be shorter but more frequent and text based. In addition, facilitators will share information through quickly created video snippets.

At the same time, learning experience facilitators will need to find the right balance. They can be always on without getting overwhelmed. They'll need to master the art of communicating regularly with participants while managing their time. Success will be measured by their ability to maximize the availability of technology while minimizing any of its potential downfalls.

Specialized Tailoring

If you've shopped online for anything in the last few years, you've likely seen the "Recommended for You" section highlighting products based upon your past purchases. The idea of tailoring content based on your unique needs is nothing new. We've seen it applied in the modern LXP, which recommends courses to participants based upon their role, background knowledge, or other programs taken. To a training program participant, specialized tailoring means providing content that's a perfect fit for their distinctive learning needs at the right time with the right amount of information and practice.

What's new and next in specialized tailoring is the way a learning experience facilitator fits into this model. It's bringing this tailored approach into facilitator-led learning experiences. Think of it this way: A facilitator in the past would expect a group of learners to show up for class and move through the learning topics according to the prescribed agenda. The facilitator may have researched the audience in advance to select relevant stories and practice examples, but they largely led the learning experience according to their plan and timetable.

To illustrate, many years ago I was facilitating a blended leadership program for a well-known global manufacturing company. The four-month curriculum included a few traditional classroom programs along with virtual events, self-led e-learning, reflection assignments, and individual coaching. I spent most of my preparation time planning for the traditional classroom portions, planning my stories and scripting the activities. I tailored the content to the organization and was confident it would be just what they needed. But I was discouraged by my participants, who were senior leaders, who seemed uninterested and distracted during our time together. Everything changed, however, when I met with them individually during the 1:1 coaching sessions. I got to know each person on a deeper level as we talked about their current challenges and how the leadership lessons applied directly to them. We built a trusted relationship by talking about their specific day-to-day issues. And they came to life as we discussed applying new techniques and strategies to find solutions. Their learning took priority.

This situation was a great reminder to me that in the midst of a carefully choreographed and well-designed program, what mattered most was the individual learner.

The learning experience facilitator of the future will meet learners where they are. They will recognize each participant's unique circumstances and use their coaching and supporting skills to enable learning on their level. Instead of participants coming to the facilitator on cue, the facilitator will show up for participants. It may be in a formal setting like a new-hire orientation program, or more likely it will be through a learning path with touchpoints along the way. However, this tailored learning isn't the result of an algorithm—it's the result of a relationship.

If you're reading this section and thinking, "But how do we customize training programs with a personal touch without relying on technology? We have to scale our solutions," you are asking the wrong question. A better question to ask is, "How do we best support the individuals who need to learn with facilitator guidance?" It's about an abundance mentality instead of a scarcity mentality. It's about getting smart with resources to support what's needed. With this mindset, you will discover ample ways to make it happen. For example, can you include additional self-discovery activities on a learning path to answer frequently asked questions? Or could you partner up experienced learners with novices so they can rely on each other during a program, in addition to receiving facilitator support? Or could you reorganize your facilitator team to accommodate varying working hours?

In the midst of my observations and predictions for the learning experience facilitator role, what will not change is the importance of human relationships. The interpersonal skills necessary to show respect, build rapport, and make others feel valued will always take center stage for a successful facilitator. The ability to read emotion and respond with genuine empathy remains a hallmark of success—especially when participants may be vulnerable as they learn new skills and try new things. The ability to meet someone where they are in a nuanced state and help them overcome obstacles that get in the way of their success—that is the quality of a master facilitator, both now and in the future.

Finding Your Path

I've been a facilitator all my life and I'm still learning how to do it well. That's the key to growth. To never give up the quest to learn more. And my desire to continually learn and share information has manifested in writing books like this one.

Following are three categories of recommendations that I've curated to help you learn and grow as a facilitator. Implement them all or pick the ones that most closely align to your current situation.

Start Where You Are—Take the Next Step

Some of you might be thinking, "Wait a minute, just becoming a learning experience facilitator is futuristic enough for me!" The concepts presented in earlier chapters are already a stretch for me and my organization. I'm overwhelmed and have such a long journey ahead of me to catch up.

If that's where you are along your growth path, it's completely fine! The predictions and recommendations in this chapter are here to help you evolve, flourish, and stay abreast of future trends. Start here and see if you can leapfrog ahead. Growth isn't a linear process. Be open to change and embrace new methods. Your willingness to try—as evidenced by reading this book—will carry you much of the way.

First, begin with why you might not be up to speed on current facilitator techniques. Are you simply a creature of habit? Or do you typically resist change? Maybe you have always facilitated this way, and because it's worked enough to get by, you haven't had a reason to change. Or maybe you have just been so busy with work or life that you haven't taken the time to notice what's going on in the industry. Perhaps the organization you work for has limited technology or other resources. Regardless of the reason, now is the time to break out of your rut. It's time for new adventures and new habits. One step at a time, or maybe one giant leap at a time!

Next, consider simple things you can do to grow as a facilitator. Maybe it's something like coming up with three thought-provoking questions to ask in the first 30 minutes of your next class. Or asking a more experienced facilitator to join you for an observation and feedback session.

In addition to reviewing the information in this book, another place to start is with ATD's Talent Development Capability Model. It's our profession's standard guide to what facilitators need to know and do. Review the Training Delivery & Facilitation Section of the model to select one thing you will incorporate into your practice (ATD 2020a).

Look for actions that help you move from lecture to conversation or from telling to asking. Another way to think about it is to release control to your learners. As a self-professed control freak right here, I won't sugarcoat this for you. It's hard. Relinquishing control to learners may feel like you're not doing your job. But the best way to help your participants is to get out of their way and let them learn. For example, if you're leading a class and following a script, ask your learners, "Which of these topics would you like to focus on first?" Then adapt your delivery plan based on their feedback. You're not skipping over content; you're just allowing the participants to take the lead.

Here are some additional practical tips on how to up your skills as a learning experience facilitator:

- **Join a networking group.** Invite colleagues from your local community to meet or join an online group of facilitators. There are a plethora of online facilitator communities waiting for your contribution and connection.
- **Create a practice roundtable.** Ask each person to bring something to share, such as a new tool, a lesson learned, or an experience.
- **Read.** Read again and read some more. Establish a book club with colleagues to explore new titles and topics.
- **Find a mentor.** Reach out to someone more experienced than you for networking or conversation. Or try a reverse mentorship—one where the mentor is younger or less experienced than you. You may be surprised at how much you can learn from each other.

- **Initiate a self-review.** Do a gap analysis on your current facilitation skills. Ask trusted advisors for honest feedback, and apply the suggestions received.
- **Treat problems as learning opportunities.** Discover new solutions by looking at challenges from a new perspective. Lessons-learned meetings are a fantastic growth opportunity.
- **Partner with another facilitator.** Co-facilitate programs and learn from their experience.
- **Start small.** Go one change at a time. Pilot one new program using the new facilitation skills learned. See how it goes and build from there.

Implementing these techniques is good for any facilitator, especially those looking to get up to speed.

Stay Current

My now eight-year-old son is learning English grammar in elementary school, and it's been a good reminder for me of the basic principles. For example, a word ending in -*ing* is typically a verb, specifically a present participle. Its ending implies ongoing motion. So, to say "I am sitting in a chair" means that I am currently sitting down in it, and to say "Jon is speaking" means that he is talking at this present moment.

However, there are also nouns that end in -*ing*, like running or surfing. These are called gerunds. A sentence example could be "Running is fun!" which makes perfect sense and follows English-language rules to be a complete sentence.

I think it's no mistake that the world *learning* is a gerund, and thus similar to a present participle. "Learning" implies ongoing motion—it's something we do and continue to do, past, present, and future.

So, just because you may be current right now as a facilitator doesn't mean you will stay current. At one time in my career, I was a certified expert in software programs that ran on the DOS operating system. Today, while that knowledge still serves me well, it's no longer cutting-edge information. I've needed to continue learning and growing to stay relevant.

Continuous learning doesn't happen by accident. It requires a determined resolve to invest in your own development and make it a priority. No one else is more invested in your personal and professional growth than you are. You are in charge of yourself, and you are responsible for managing your development.

Recently I heard from a training professional who attended one of my webcasts. She followed up afterward with a question and a request to chat. In that conversation I learned that she had taken the day off from work so that she could attend the webcast without interruption from her office. She wanted to learn so badly that she was willing to sacrifice a day off just for her own benefit. She invested her time into herself and those dividends will pay a future return on her investment. Hopefully her story inspires you as much as it did me.

Here are some practical ways to stay current as a learning experience facilitator:

- **Initiate a self-review.** Periodically take stock of yourself and your personal development. When was the last time you took a formal class? Or paused for your own professional development? Earned a certification? Consider your next step in light of where you have been and where you want to go.
- **Set a goal or two.** For example, what are three things you want to learn about in the next 12 months? Write them down and then create a plan with a small milestone you can achieve. Check in with that goal every month, adjusting as needed.
- **Resolve to learn.** Most people don't keep New Year's resolutions for very long. Why? Because they say they'll do something but don't put a support structure in place to actually do it. So, make a resolution to learn, and then put measures in place to help you stick with it. Don't give up if you miss a day or week; instead, focus on progress

over perfection. Remind yourself of your plan, realign your priorities, and get back to your resolution.

- **Schedule learning.** It's been said that your wallet and your calendar will reveal your priorities. Is learning one of them? If not, carve out time in your schedule for it. Ask for help from others to keep this commitment. For me, when I schedule professional development time, I note it in my calendar as "Appointment with Sally." Anyone who sees my calendar thinks I'm meeting with another person; in reality, Sally is a childhood nickname that only my dad used. It's my way of indicating this is personal learning time. Find your own method and use that to mark time on your calendar for learning.

- **Read, read, read some more.** Be a voracious reader of quality content. Curate your content in a way that allows you to keep up and reference it. If you're like me and have limited time to read, add audiobooks to your repertoire.

- **Attend industry conferences.** Conferences are not only educational events; they're also prime opportunities to network. Cultivate relationships with other attendees. When planning out your conference schedule, include dine-arounds and other social events. Or simply strike up a conversation with people sitting near you in a session, because they obviously share similar interests.

- **Connect with a professional association.** Most associations have multiple ways to get involved. Start by joining your local or regional chapter. Invest in a membership to the national or global levels. Find a volunteer opportunity to contribute, and you'll likely gain so much more in return.

- **Subscribe to industry journals.** This is where you'll find new authors, writing about new trends. Look for patterns and buzzwords. While not all buzzwords turn into lasting trends, it's always interesting to see what's on the mind of publishers who make a business of seeking new and fresh content.

- **Experiment with new technologies.** Raise your hand to volunteer when offered the opportunity to try new things. Become a beta tester for new programs. Be open to experimenting with technology as a learning experience.
- **Partner with your organization.** If you're internal to the business, partner with your manager for learning opportunities. Take on stretch projects. Let company leadership know of your interest in growth and learning. If you're external, partner with trusted clients or your professional association.

By taking an intentional approach to learning, you will stay current and stay relevant as a learning experience facilitator.

Stay Ahead

What about looking forward and staying ahead of the curve? You may want to be a facilitator who doesn't just stay current but also stays cutting edge. To do this, you'll want to look for places to find future trends and strategies to keep your skills fresh and forward looking.

Many futuristic concepts are grounded in current reality. It's rare for any industry to see a true market disruptor (such as what the iPod did for music). Instead, many future trends begin with a small swell of support and grow from there. So, by simply paying attention, you may be able to catch the wave before it takes over.

On the flip side, it's easy to get caught up in shiny object syndrome. Just because something is all the rage or deemed buzzworthy doesn't make it the next big thing—it could be like cotton candy, only fluff without any substance.

I absolutely love following future trends and am always thinking about possibilities. Here are my recommendations for keeping your eye on the future of facilitation:

- **Commit to being a lifelong learner.** It's a theme from earlier in this chapter that can't be overemphasized or over-repeated. Never stop learning or being open to new ideas.
- **Pay attention to other industries.** Many future trends begin in business, outside the learning industry. Read newspapers and business journals, especially technology-related ones. Ask yourself how new items might influence your ways of working if they showed up in your day-to-day activities.
- **Subscribe to vendor marketing lists.** While you might not enjoy the extra email, you'll be the first to find out about new products and new features. Pay attention to these new innovations.
- **Practice deep reflection.** When I need to think or reflect, I tune out the noise around me and move to my quiet thinking chair. This corner of my home office is set up with minimal distractions, just a pen and pad of paper. It's the place where I sit when I need to concentrate and ponder what's going on around me. I attribute my ability to think to having this one spot where I intentionally go. What's your place?

VOICES FROM THE FIELD

"Staying current as a professional is getting more challenging because there is so much to keep up with, and work has gotten more demanding than ever. I like to attend the annual ATD conference, as well as a few webinars throughout the month that are focused on new-to-me topics or skills I want to refine. I at least skim *TD* magazine and invitations to other conferences to see what the hot topics are. Truly, one of the most important things I do is keep facilitating! I make sure I facilitate regularly, review materials and practice before each session, and listen to what participants say is happening in their organizations. I then look into topics they mention if I haven't heard about them. This ensures I stay on top of my game."
—**Sharon Wingron, CEO, DevelopPEOPLE**

Final Thoughts: Stay Connected

No matter what comes down the road for facilitation, my best advice is to remember that it's about people. Technology will advance and methods will evolve. The only thing we can be absolutely sure of is that change will happen, but in the end what matters is our relationships. Keep your eyes on others and how you can best serve them. This desire will carry you to the next level of facilitation.

Finally, I invite you to stay connected with me. I've created a resource page on my website that will help us all stay current on trends and connect with one another (Figure 8-1; cindyhuggett.com/facilitatorsguide). This resource page already includes some of the ready-to-use items found in this book. My site also serves as a go-to place for your questions and comments about facilitation skills. I hope to hear from you and learn from your experiences as well. Let's learn from each other.

FIGURE 8-1. Scan to Stay in Touch!

Acknowledgments

This book would not have been possible without the support and encouragement from others, and these brief words of recognition only skim the surface of my overwhelming thanks to everyone who helped me in the process.

First, a special thanks to the many business and training professionals who willingly shared their experiences, advice, and stories, including Carrie Addington, Nanci Appleman-Vassil, Scott Cooksey, Jessica DeCanio, Angelle Lafrance, Sardék Love, Maureen Orey, Howard Prager, Marion Schilcher, Nikki Ryan, Kathy Shurte, Bill Treasurer, Christie Ward, and Sharon Wingron, along with a few who chose to remain anonymous. (You know who you are!) I am appreciative to each one of them for their willingness to offer wisdom and their lessons learned. Their contributions have greatly enriched this book. Thank you.

I'm also extremely grateful for several individuals who reviewed portions and early versions of the manuscript, including Elaine Biech, Betty Dannewitz, Destery Hillenbrand, Kristen Torrence, and Connie Malamed. Special thanks also goes to Sherri Stotler for her incredible research and organizational skills, to Marilyn Wright for helping get some of my thoughts down on the page, to Keri DeDeo for her incredible editing support, and to Betty Dannewitz for creating the AR experiences throughout this book. All of their insights were invaluable and made this book much better than it would have been otherwise.

Thank you also to the entire ATD team—especially Justin Brusino, Alexandria Clapp, Jack Harlow, Hannah Sternberg, and Melissa Jones—for their enormous patience during the lengthy book writing process. Their encouragement and advice carried this book through from concept to completion. Melissa's skill in editing and her mastery with words deserves special attention. She is a gift to authors.

Finally, I dedicate this book to Bobby and Jonathan. It was because of their love and support that this book was finished.

Cindy Huggett
Psalm 115:1
December 2022

Recommended Resources

I encourage you to continue studying the topics covered throughout this book. If you are interested in diving deeper, here are a few resources I recommend. This list represents a wide variety of topics, ranging from traditional training and development to technology to business, and everything in between. Enjoy the journey of exploration!

Elaine Biech, ed., *ATD's Handbook for Training & Talent Development* (Alexandria, VA: ATD Press, 2022).

Elaine Biech, *The Art and Science of Training* (Alexandria, VA: ATD Press, 2016).

Robert O. Brinkerhoff, Anne M. Apking, and Edward W. Boon, *Improving Performance Through Learning: A Practical Guide for Designing High Performance Learning Journeys* (Independently published, 2019).

Brandon Carson, *L&D's Playbook for the Digital Age* (Alexandria, VA: ATD Press, 2021).

Darlene Christopher, *The Successful Virtual Classroom: How to Design and Facilitate Interactive and Engaging Live Online Learning* (New York: AMACOM, 2014).

Ruth Colvin Clark, *Evidence-Based Training Methods*, 3rd ed. (Alexandria, VA: ATD Press, 2019).

Ruth Colvin Clark and Richard E. Mayer, *e-Learning and the Science of Instruction: Proven Guidelines for Consumers and Designers of Multimedia Learning*, 4th ed. (Hoboken, NJ: Wiley, 2016).

Cynthia Clay, *Great Webinars: How to Create Interactive Learning That Is Captivating, Informative, and Fun* (Punchy Publishing, 2019).

Julie Dirksen, *Design for How People Learn*, 2nd ed. (Berkeley, CA: New Riders, 2015).

Jaime Donally, *Learning Transported: Augmented, Virtual and Mixed Reality for All Classrooms* (Portland, OR: International Society for Technology in Education, 2018).

Jaime Donally, *The Immersive Classroom: Create Customized Learning Experiences With AR/VR* (Portland, OR: International Society for Technology in Education, 2021).

Tamar Elkeles, Jack J. Phillips, and Patricia P. Phillips. *Measuring the Success of Learning Through Technology: A Guide for Measuring Impact and Calculating ROI on E-Learning, Blended Learning, and Mobile Learning* (Alexandria, VA: ATD Press, 2014).

Cathy Hackl and John Buzzell, *The Augmented Workforce: How AR, AI & 5G Will Impact Every Dollar You Make* (Renown Publishing, 2021).

Jonathan Halls, *Rapid Media Development for Trainers* (Alexandria, VA: ATD Press, 2016).

Jennifer Hofmann, *Blended Learning* (Alexandria, VA: ATD Press, 2018).

Diana L. Howles, *Next Level Virtual Training: Advance Your Facilitation* (Alexandria, VA: ATD Press, 2022).

Cindy Huggett, *The Virtual Training Guidebook: How to Design, Deliver, and Implement Live Online Learning* (Alexandria, VA: ATD Press, 2013).

Cindy Huggett, *Virtual Training Tools and Templates: An Action Guide to Live Online Learning* (Alexandria, VA: ATD Press, 2017).

Micah Jacobson and Mari Ruddy, *Open to Outcome: A Practical Guide for Facilitating and Teaching Experiential Reflection*, 2nd ed. (Bethany, OK: Wood N. Barnes, 2015).

Kassy LaBorie, *Producing Virtual Training, Meetings, and Webinars: Master the Technology to Engage Participants* (Alexandria, VA: ATD Press, 2020).

Kassy LaBorie and Tom Stone, *Interact and Engage!: 75+ Activities for Virtual Training, Meetings, and Webinars*, 2nd ed. (Alexandria, VA: ATD Press, 2022).

Margie Meacham, *AI in Talent Development* (Alexandria, VA: ATD Press, 2020).

Patricia P. Phillips, ed., *ASTD Handbook of Measuring and Evaluating Training* (Alexandria, VA: ATD Press, 2010).

Robert W. Pike, *Master Trainer Handbook: Tips, Tactics, and How-Tos for Delivering Effective Instructor-Led, Participant-Centered Training*, 4th ed. (Amherst, MA: HRD Press, 2015).

Becky Pike Pluth, *Creative Training: A Train-the-Trainer Field Guide* (Minneapolis, MN: Creative Training Productions, 2016).

Clark N. Quinn, *Learning Science for Instructional Designers* (Alexandria, VA: ATD Press, 2021).

Karin M. Reed and Joseph A. Allen, *Suddenly Hybrid: Managing the Modern Meeting* (Hoboken, NJ: John Wiley & Sons, 2022).

Brian Washburn, *What's Your Formula? Combine Learning Elements for Impactful Training* (Alexandria, VA: ATD Press, 2021).

References

Alexander, A., R. Cracknell, A. De Smet, M. Langstaff, M. Mysore, and D. Ravid. 2021. "What Executives Are Saying about the Future of Hybrid Work." McKinsey & Company, May 17. mckinsey.com/business -functions/people-and-organizational-performance/our-insights /what-executives-are-saying-about-the-future-of-hybrid-work.

Alsop, T. n.d. "Augmented reality (AR), virtual reality (VR), and mixed reality (MR) market size worldwide in 2021 and 2028." Statista, accessed November 23, 2021. statista.com/statistics/591181/global-augmented -virtual-reality-market-size.

Association for Talent Development (ATD). 2020a. *2020 State of the Industry*. Alexandria, VA: ATD Press.

Association for Talent Development (ATD). 2020b. Talent Development Body of Knowledge. Alexandria, VA: ATD.

Association for Talent Development (ATD). 2021. *Virtual Classrooms: Leveraging Technology for Impact*. Alexandria, VA: ATD Press.

Autor, D.H., and B. Price. 2013. "The Changing Task Composition of the US Labor Market: An Update of Autor, Levy, and Murnane (2003)." *MIT Economics*, June 21. economics.mit.edu/files/9758.

Bersin, J. 2019. "VR Enters Corporate Learning With a Vengeance: And the Results Are Amazing." Josh Bersin, January 27; updated March 9, 2021. joshbersin.com/2019/01/vr-enters-corporate-learning-with-a -vengeance-and-the-results-are-amazing.

Bliss-Moreau, E., M.J. Owren, and L.F. Barrett. 2010. "I Like the Sound of Your Voice: Affective Learning About Vocal Signals." *Journal of Experimental Social Psychology* 46(3): 557–63. doi.org/10.1016/j .jesp.2009.12.017.

Brown, E. 2019. "Over Half of Consumers Will Choose a Chatbot Over a Human to Save Time." ZDNet, January 2. zdnet.com/article /over-half-of-consumers-will-choose-a-chatbot-over-a-human-to-save -time.

Burstein, D. 2015. "Email Marketing Chart: Personalized Subject Lines." MarketingSherpa, June 16. marketingsherpa.com/article/chart /personal-subject-lines.

Chernikova, O., N. Heitzmann, M. Stadler, D. Holzberger, T. Seidel, and F. Fischer. 2020. "Simulation-Based Learning in Higher Education: A Meta-Analysis." *Review of Educational Research* 90(4): 499–541. doi .org/10.3102/0034654320933544.

Cisco. n.d. "Webex Hologram." Cisco Project Workplace, accessed March 28, 2022. projectworkplace.cisco.com/capabilities/hologram.

Clark, R.C. 2020. *Evidence-Based Training Methods: A Guide for Training Professionals*, 3rd ed. Alexandria, VA: ATD Press.

Clark, R.C., and R.E. Mayer. 2016. "Applying the Personalization and Embodiment Principles: Use Conversational Style, Polite Wording, Human Voice, and Virtual Coaches." Chapter 9 in *e-Learning and the Science of Instruction*, edited by R.C. Clark and R.E. Mayer. Hoboken, NJ: John Wiley & Sons.

Dannewitz, B. 2020. "Pop-Up AR: How a Fitness Facility Implemented AR for Safety Training (Betty Dannewitz)." Professional Association for Computer Training, October 9. pactmn.org/product/pop-up -ar-how-a-fitness-facility-implemented-ar-for-safety-training.

Driscoll, J., and B. Teh. 2001. "The Potential of Reflective Practice to Develop Individual Orthopaedic Nurse Practitioners and Their Practice." *Journal of Orthopaedic Nursing* 5(2): 95–103. doi.org/10.1054 /joon.2001.0150.

Good News Translation (GNT). American Bible Society. biblegateway.com /versions/Good-News-Translation-GNT-Bible.

Hall, MJ, and D. Holt. 2018. "Learning at the Moment of Need." ATD blog, November 1. td.org/insights/learning-at-the-moment-of-need.

Hudson, C.C., and V.R. Whisler. 2008. "Contextual Teaching and Learning for Practitioners." *Journal of Systemics, Cybernetics, and Informatics* 6(4): 54–58.

Huggett, C. 2010. *Virtual Training Basics*. Alexandria, VA: ATD Press.

Huggett, C. 2014. *The Virtual Training Guidebook: How to Design, Deliver, and Implement Live Online Learning*. Alexandria, VA: ATD Press.

Huggett, C. 2016. *Virtual Training Tools and Templates: An Action Guide to Live Online Learning*. Alexandria, VA: ATD Press.

Huggett, C. 2021. "The State of Virtual Training 2022." Cindy Huggett blog, December 7. cindyhuggett.com/blog/2022sovt.

Jaehnig, J. 2021. "SAP, JFF Labs, and Talespin Launch Skill Immersion Lab for Immersive Learning Soft Skills." *ARPost*, October 12. arpost .co/2021/10/12/skill-immersion-lab-immersive-learning.

James, D. 2020. "Workflow Learning and the 5 Moments of Need With Bob Mosher." *The Learning & Development Podcast*, October 28. amazon.com /Workflow-Learning-Moments-Need-Mosher/dp/B08KVB7CY8.

Khan, T., K. Johnston, and J. Ophoff. 2019. "The Impact of an Augmented Reality Application on Learning Motivation of Students." *Advances in Human-Computer Interaction 2019*. doi.org/10.1155/2019/7208494.

King, A. 1993. "From Sage on the Stage to Guide on the Side." *College Teaching* 41(1): 30–35.

Kolb, D.A. 1984. *Experimental Learning: Experience as the Source of Learning and Development*. Englewood Cliffs, CO: Prentice-Hall.

Leading Effectively Staff. 2020. "Immediately Improve Talent Development With Our SBI Feedback Model." Center for Creative Leadership (CCL), November 24. ccl.org/articles/leading-effectively-articles/sbi-feedback -model-a-quick-win-to-improve-talent-conversations-development.

"Learning." Dictionary.com, accessed March 28, 2022. dictionary.com /browse/learning.

Lefrak, M. 2022. "Want to Smell in Virtual Reality? A Vermont-Based Startup Has the Technology." WBUR News, March 14. wbur.org/news /2022/03/14/virtual-reality-smell-ovr-technology.

Likens, S., and D.L. Eckert. 2021. "How Virtual Reality Is Redefining Soft Skills Training." PwC, June 4. pwc.com/us/en/tech-effect/emerging -tech/virtual-reality-study.html.

Malamed, C. 2022. "10 Principles of Learning Experience Design." The eLearning Coach, March 12. theelearningcoach.com/lxd/10-principles -of-lxd.

Matchar, E. 2018. "Using Electric Currents to Fool Ourselves Into Tasting Something We're Not." *Smithsonian Magazine*, August 15. smithsonianmag.com/innovation/using-electric-currents-to-fool -ourselves-into-tasting-something-were-not-180970005.

Mayer, R.E. 2014. "Principles Based on Social Cues in Multimedia Learning: Personalization, Voice, Image, and Embodiment Principles." Chapter 14 in *The Cambridge Handbook of Multimedia Learning*, 2nd ed., edited by R.E. Mayer. New York: Cambridge University Press.

McKeachie, W.J. 2014. *McKeachie's Teaching Tips: Strategies, Research, and Theory for College and University Teachers*, 14th ed. Australia: Wadsworth, Cengage Learning.

McKinlay, T. 2021. "High Quality Audio Makes You Sound Smarter." Ariyh, April 15. tips.ariyh.com/p/good-sound-quality-smarter?s=r.

McKnight, K.S., and M. Scruggs. 2008. *The Second City Guide to Improv in the Classroom: Using Improvisation to Teach Skills and Boost Learning*. San Francisco: Jossey-Bass.

Min, F., Z. Fang, Y. He, and J. Xuan. 2021. "Research on Users' Trust of Chatbots Driven by AI: An Empirical Analysis Based on System Factors and User Characteristics." *2021 IEEE International Conference on Consumer Electronics and Computer Engineering (ICCECE)*. doi.org /10.1109/ICCECE51280.2021.9342098.

mursion.devops. 2020. "The Secret to Our Success: Mursion's Simulation Specialists." Mursion blog, August 4. mursion.com/products /simulation-specialists.

Oh, C.S., J.N. Bailenson, and G.F. Welch. 2018. "A Systematic Review of Social Presence: Definition, Antecedents, and Implications." *Frontiers in Robotics and AI* 5, October 15. doi.org/10.3389/frobt.2018.00114.

Pew Research Center. 2021. "Mobile Fact Sheet." Pew Research Center: Internet, Science & Tech, April 7. pewresearch.org/internet/fact-sheet/mobile.

Pi, Z., K. Xu, C. Liu, and J. Yang. 2020. "Instructor Presence in Video Lectures: Eye Gaze Matters, but Not Body Orientation." *Computers & Education* 144. doi.org/10.1016/j.compedu.2019.103713.

Santos, H.C., M.E. W. Varnum, and I. Grossmann. 2017. "Global Increases in Individualism." *Psychological Science* 28(9): 1228–1239. doi.org/10.1177/0956797617700622.

Shank, P. 2016. *The Science of Learning*. Alexandria, VA: ATD Press.

Silver, L. 2019. "Smartphone Ownership Is Growing Rapidly Around the World, but Not Always Equally." Pew Research Center, February 5. pewresearch.org/global/2019/02/05/smartphone-ownership-is-growing-rapidly-around-the-world-but-not-always-equally.

"Virtual." *Merriam-Webster*. Accessed March 28, 2022. merriam-webster.com/dictionary/virtual.

Vogels, E.A. 2020. "About One-in-Five Americans Use a Smart Watch or Fitness Tracker." Pew Research Center, January 9. pewresearch.org/fact-tank/2020/01/09/about-one-in-five-americans-use-a-smart-watch-or-fitness-tracker.

Walton, G. 2017. "Pioneering French Midwife: Angélique Du Coudray." Geri Walton, April 17. geriwalton.com/pioneering-french-midwife-angelique-du-coudray.

White, C.S. 2016. "6 Shocking Myths About Subject Lines." Litmus, October 12. litmus.com/blog/6-shocking-myths-about-subject-lines.

Yorton, T. 2013. "Showtime! Improv Tips for Training." *Training*, May 17. trainingmag.com/showtime-improv-tips-for-training.

Index

Page numbers followed by *f* and *t* refer to figures and tables, respectively.

feedback
  emoji, 43–44, 44f
  haptic, 27–28
  indicators, 41
  and nex-gen polling, 44–45
  nonverbal, 42t
  providing, 14t–15t, 52, 84, 115,
    117–118, 120–122, 135
  receiving, 39, 58–59, 112
field of view (FoV), 27
flipped classrooms, 99
French Academy of Surgeons, vi

G

Giant Leap Consulting, 161
Google Cardboard, 151
Google Glass, 33
Gottfredson, Conrad, 7–8
group dynamics, managing, 14,
  54, 57, 61–63, 73t
guided learning journeys. *See*
  blended learning journeys
"guide on the side," 5–6

H

hand-gesture recognition, 29, 42t,
  43–44, 50, 137–138, 139f
head mounted displays (HMD), 28
headsets, VR. *See* VR headsets
"help desk" mentality, 174
holograms, 127
HoloLens glasses, 34

hybrid classes, 75–96
  adapting to, 77–78
  challenges of, 76–77
  helping hands for, 80–83
  leading discussions in, 89–92
  preparing for, 78–80
  using applied knowledge in,
    83–85
  using audio in, 85–86
  using video in, 86–88
hybrid classrooms, 21–22

I

icebreakers, 55–56, 132. *See also*
  opening activities
immersion
  definition of, 27
  and interruptions, 169
  in VR, 148f
immersive learning, vi–vii, 14,
  17–36
  and augmented reality, 31–34, 35
  blended, 23
  and extended reality, 34–35
  hybrid classrooms in, 21–22
  and learning platforms, 23–25
  and mixed reality, 34, 35
  technology used in, 19–21
  and virtual reality, 25–31, 35
immersive view viewing mode, 87
immersive virtual classes, 37–73
  and current mindset, 38–40

presence, 27–28

professional capability, building, 3

Q

QR codes, 33, 34f

R

rapport, building, 54, 55–58, 73t, 87, 116, 184

Riff Analytics, 40

Robert Brinkerhoff's High-Impact Learning Journey, 99

role playing, 4, 10, 27, 83, 103, 145, 173

round robin "report out" method, 66

S

"sage on the stage," 5–6

Sardek Love International, 137

SBI model (Center for Creative Leadership), 171

scavenger hunts, 132

Schilcher, Marion, 18

screen sharing, 42t

"seat time." *See* learning time

self-directed learning, 6, 11, 178

as asynchronous events, 19

in blended learning journeys, 106–108

and communication, 116–117

facilitator-led vs., 139–140

navigating, 121

simulation sages, 166–168

Siri, 155

six degrees of freedom (6DoF), 27

Skill Immersion Lab (SAP), 155–156

SnapChat Spectacles, 33

Spatial (VR meeting room), 153

specialized tailoring, 182–184

Star Trek, 26

State of Virtual Training 2022 survey, 38, 47

storytelling, 14t–15t, 15

subject matter experts (SMEs), 13

synchronous learning events, 19–20, 22

T

Talent Development Capability Model (ADT), 3–4, 11, 121, 186

Teaching Tips (McKeachie), 1

technology

immersive, 10, 34–35

for immersive learning, 17–36

overview of, 19–21

ubiquitous, 180–182

of VR controllers, 29

360-degree audio, 163

360-degree video, 28

Three degrees of freedom (3DoF), 4

time-saving efficiencies, 101–103

About the Author

Cindy Huggett is a pioneer in the field of online learning with more than 20 years of experience in providing virtual training solutions and more than 30 years in the world of talent development. She's a leading industry expert known for teaching thousands of training professionals how to design and deliver practical, engaging interactive online classes to today's global workforce through workshops, speaking, coaching, and consulting. Cindy partners with organizations to upskill facilitators, maximize online learning design, and facilitate actionable learning solutions that meet today's needs and leverage tomorrow's technologies.

Cindy has written several acclaimed books on virtual training, including *Virtual Training Tools and Templates: An Action Guide to Live Online Learning; The Virtual Training Guidebook: How to Design, Deliver, and Implement Live Online Learning;* and *Virtual Training Basics.* She's the co-author of two *Infoline* issues and a contributor to many other industry publications, including *TD* magazine and the third edition of *ATD's Handbook for Training and Talent Development.*

A sought-after conference speaker, Cindy has presented multiple times at the ATD International Conference & EXPO, TechKnowledge, Training, DevLearn, TechLearn, Learning, and the annual SHRM Conference. Her online webcasts have been attended by thousands of people around the globe. She's one of only a handful of worldwide facilitators originally chosen to deliver ATD's Master Trainer and Master Instructional Designer Programs.

Throughout her career, Cindy has worked in various industries, including technology, construction, higher education, retail, and the public sector. Her management and global experience include serving as the regional director of training and operations for an international software training company, and the learning and development manager for a global mechanical contractor.

Cindy holds a master's degree in public and international affairs from the University of Pittsburgh and a bachelor's degree from James Madison University. She was also one of the first to earn the prestigious Certified Professional in Learning and Performance (CPLP, now CPTD) designation. Cindy is a past member of the global ATD Board of Directors, was recognized by the *Triangle Business Journal* as a 40-Under-40 Award recipient, and co-founded a nonprofit organization to promote volunteering and community service in her local area. She's also a yoga teacher with a special focus on mobility for aging seniors. She's passionate about service and helping others.

Outside the classroom, you can typically find Cindy at home in Raleigh, North Carolina, sipping a cup of hot English breakfast tea, spending time with her hockey-loving son and husband, or cheering on her favorite teams—especially her beloved Pittsburgh teams (Steelers, Pirates, Penguins) and, of course, the Carolina Hurricanes.